SPRING SUMMER 2004
WWW.PAULSMITH.CO.UK

look at your work we'd love to
look at your work we'd love to
look at your work we'd love t
look at your work we'd love
look at your work we'd love
to look at your work we'd love
to look at your work we'd lov
to look at your work we'd lo
to look at your work we'd lo
look at your work we'd lo

mail graphic@magmabooks.com
ail graphic@magmabooks.com
ail graphic@magmabooks.co
ail graphic@magmabooks.co
ail graphic@magmabooks.c
mail graphic@magmabooks.c
email graphic@magmabooks.
mail graphic@magmabooks.
email graphic@magmabooks
mail graphic@magmabooks

Graphic Magazine
Issue Four

Editors
Marc-A Valli
    Editor-in-Chief
    marc@magmabooks.com
Lachlan Blackley
    Features Editor
    lachlan@magmabooks.com
Samuel Baker
Sebastian Campos
Mairi Duthie
Inca Starzinsky

Design
Samuel Baker
Sebastian Campos (Aficionado)
Inca Starzinsky

Publisher
Rudolf van Wezel

Production
Sylvia van de Poel

Advertising & Marketing
Mairi Duthie
T +44 7780 707 004

Printing
Drukkerij Tuijtel
Hardinxveld-Giessendam
The Netherlands

Paper
For this edition the paper choice has
been selected from the international
assortment of Schneider Papier
Benelux. For more information please
visit www.schneider-papier.nl

Luxocard I, 250gsm
    Cover
BVS Plus Gloss, 150gsm
    pp1–48, 81–112, 145–160
Planospeed, 120gsm, volume 1.32
    pp49–80
Chorus Semi Matt, 150gsm
    pp113–144
Recystar, 150 gsm, volume 1.30
    pp161–176
Trockengummiert Offset, 80gsm
    Inserted stamps

Insert: People / Places / Things
Design: Alon Levin
Image Source: Artreference 3
Verlags–und Lizenzgesellschaft mbH
Germany 1979

Addresses

Editorial
Graphic Magazine
c/o Magma
117–119 Clerkenwell Road
London, EC1R 5BY
United Kingdom
T +44 20 7242 9522
F +44 20 7242 9504
graphic@magmabooks.com
www.magmabooks.com

Publishing, Subscriptions
and Advertising
BIS Publishers
Herengracht 370–372
NL-1016 CH Amsterdam
The Netherlands
T +31 20 524 75 60
F +31 20 524 75 57
graphic@bispublishers.nl
www.bispublishers.nl

BISPUBLISHERS

Subscription rates
(all prices include airmail)

1 year (4 issues)
    Europe: EUR80/£55
    USA / Canada: US$105
    Other countries: US$125

2 years (8 issues)
    Europe: EUR149/£103
    USA / Canada: US$195
    Other countries: US$225

Student subscription
(valid only with a copy of your
student registration form)

1 year (4 issues)
    Europe: EUR63/£43.50
    USA / Canada: US$90
    Other countries: US$100

How to subscribe?
Use the subscription card in the
magazine or mail, fax or e-mail
us your name, company name,
(delivery) address, country &
telephone / fax number and the type
of subscription you require. Please
include details of your credit card
type, number, expiry date and your
signature. If paying by Mastercard,
please also add the CVC-2 code (last
3 digits of the number printed on the
signature strip of the credit card). If
the delivery address is not the same
as the credit card's billing address
please also state the billing address.
If you do not wish to pay by credit
card please mention that you wish to
receive an invoice. Your subscription
will start after payment is received.

A BIS Publishers Publication

The utmost care has been taken to
present the information in Graphic
as accurately as possible. For any
damage that may result from use
of that information neither the
publisher nor the authors can be held
responsible. All efforts have been
made to contact copyright holders.
Questions can be directed to: Graphic,
Amsterdam, the Netherlands.

ISSN 1569-4119
ISBN 90-6369-083-5

Copyright © 2004
BIS Publishers
Amsterdam, The Netherlands

George Bush Meets Dr Strangelove

by Marc-A Valli

Hello World.

Imagine a scene in a movie.

EXTERIOR, ROAD. The light is dim, either because it's still early in the morning or because it's already late in the afternoon. A bus appears on the road. It's a school bus and it's heading full speed towards a brick wall.

INTERIOR, BUS. The children are screaming, not out of fear, but with excitement. All of them are clean, well fed and well brought-up kids. But in a group they seem positively deranged, leaping up and down on their seats, incessantly teasing their neighbours, occasionally kissing or hugging someone and not that occasionally poking or punching someone. At regular intervals one of them starts wailing.

MEANWHILE, the bus is drawing ever closer to the wall.

CLOSE UP, BOY. He stops screaming and looks up from his seat. He's staring out the window, frowning. Has he noticed something? He opens one of his exercise books, scribbles something down, re-reads what he has written, before tearing the page, crunching it into a ball and aiming it at a colleague. A secret message? We will never know. The blotted ball of paper will never be unfolded. It will be thrown back, in retaliation, as soon as it has hit its target. And is then thrown again, at another target, and then in turn...

CLOSE UP, DRIVER. A small middle-aged man with a baseball cap hunched up by the wheel. He turns to a little girl sitting near him and mumbles a few incoherent words in a strong Texan accent. Then he looks back. He appears to be more interested in the action taking place in the back of the bus than on the road. There is something peculiarly childish about this man. He still indulges in juvenile fantasies – fancying himself a cowboy, the sheriff. He's like a child trying to imitate an adult, probably his father. He doesn't strike you as being bright, to say the least, and it is surprising that he should have been given such responsibility. Would you trust your children's lives in this man's hands?

THE WALL continues to grow ahead of him. It looks big and dark and daunting.

INTERIOR, GIRL. As a good little girl she can't help pointing out the danger to the driver. But he dismisses the idea as ludicrous, hysterical horseshit – and accelerates. They pass by signs on the side of the road. Unmistakable signs, every one of them spelling DANGER! in a graphic language. You wouldn't have to be educated or even literate to read these messages.

But the driver chooses to ignore them and, as the bus continues to accelerate, he can't resist whooping, 'Yiiiraaah!' while slapping the front panel with his cap. He has never hit a wall before and is possibly even looking forward to it.

CLOSE UP of the driver as he turns to the back of the bus and waves at what he calls his 'folks'. The children in the back are still leaping and screaming and laughing. The driver interprets this as a sign of his growing popularity and, clearly sharing in his 'folks' enthusiasm, he goes on whooping 'YIIIRAAAHH!' and slapping the panel with his baseball cap.

CLOSE UP of bricks on the wall. The driver can now clearly distinguish the wall's texture.

CLOSE UP of the driver's face. His eyebrows raised, his mouth shaped like an 'o', as if about to say 'Folks, I –' A thought might have finally crossed his mind. We will never know, because just at that moment a pair of small and over-excited little hands creeps up from behind to cover his eyes.

GUESS who this is?

IN SLOW MOTION, almost reluctantly, the school bus hits its target, instantly becoming as crunched up as that blotted ball of paper. It too will remain unfolded.

THE END

NO titles run over the burning debris and the billowing smoke.

Imagine a scene in real life.

*   *   *

Goodbye World.

Inside /
George Bush Meets…

Inside /
page 3

Inside /
Editorial

graphic
The environments issue

inbox
Show / Tell / Profile

OUTSIDE/PEOPLE   OUTSIDE/THINGS

inbox
Discuss / Write / Comment

OUTSIDE/PEOPLE   OUTSIDE/PLACES   OUTSIDE/THINGS

inbox
Look / Read / Use

GRIFFIN

oki-ni
25 savile row
london
w1s 3pr

birmingham life
leeds flannels
manchester flannels
nottingham flannels
glasgow cruise

oki-ni.com

oki-ni

exclusive rare product for men and women on-line

BIG
MAGAZ
...E

Big
detroit issue no. 48
bigmagazine.com
printed in chile

us $18
canada 20
france 25
germany 22
italy 18
uk £14

Show /
Tell /
Profile

OUTSIDE/PEOPLE

OUTSIDE/PLACES

OUTSIDE/THINGS

OUTSIDE/PEOPLE

OUTSIDE/PLACES

OUTSIDE/THINGS

OUTSIDE/PEOPLE

OUTSIDE/PLACES

OUTSIDE/THINGS

'SO IT WAS JUST
AN OBSESSION FROM
THAT POINT ONWARDS
UNTIL I ACTUALLY
SAT DOWN TO DO IT
AND REALISED
HOW DIFFICULT IT WAS
AND THOUGHT "OH ..."'

Marc Craste, page 32

T-Shirt Survey
Part One / 2K By Gingham

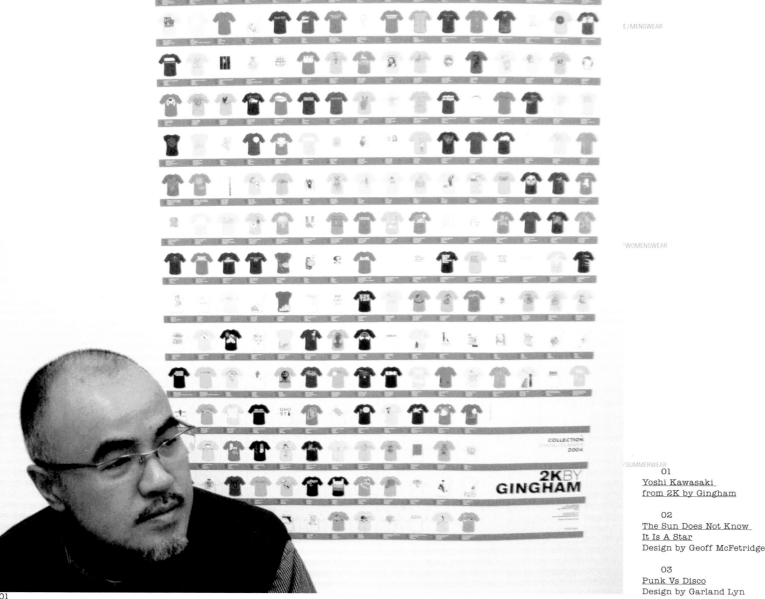

E/MENSWEAR

'WOMENSWEAR

/SUMMERWEAR

01
Yoshi Kawasaki
from 2K by Gingham

02
The Sun Does Not Know
It Is A Star
Design by Geoff McFetridge

03
Punk Vs Disco
Design by Garland Lyn

01

AN INTERVIEW WITH YOSHI KAWASAKI FROM 2K/GINGHAM

When I think t-shirts I think Gingham/2K/Yoshi. I don't know of anyone who has commissioned so many great t-shirts from visual artists as Yoshi Kawasaki. He is in the unique position of being able to travel around the world commissioning and selling t-shirts by artists and designers. The Designers Republic, Yoshitomo Nara, Graphic Havoc, Geoff McFetridge, Alex Rich, Experimental Jetset, Automatic, Alex Aranovich, M/M... It's a very nice line-up. So it seemed apt to begin this survey by talking to Yoshi.

MARC VALLI: Why t-shirts? Why a t-shirt and not a poster or a postcard? YOSHI KAWASAKI: Our company, Gingham Inc. has been in fashion industry over 20 years so it was a natural direction to use t-shirts as a canvas for our creative pursuits. **Were you an artist or designer? What were you doing before working with Gingham/2K?** No. My background is music, instead. I used to make my living playing piano, mostly jazz and blues in night clubs and lounges. **So how did you begin your involvement with graphics, art and t-shirts?** In the early 90s, many museum and popular art design

t-shirts began to be displayed in fashion boutiques in Japan. We then thought that we could compliment this current trend by researching museums throughout the world. This led us to a trip to the U.S. in 1995, to visit various museum stores in order to export and distribute their t-shirts in Japan. At that time, our most favourite design was Gilbert and George's t-shirt from the Philadelphia Museum of Art. In the meantime, frustration surfaced as we could only find a few new images that we really liked. The majority of museum t-shirts were too mainstream for us and it was becoming difficult to find contemporary cutting edge designs. At the same time we felt that the area between contemporary art and subcultures was disappearing; yet the mutual links could not be denied. These feelings brought us to start working with a variety of 'new' artists and design sources to produce 2K's own art and subculture image t-shirt line.

How did you start the company? Where? When? What's the story behind it? Gingham is not my company and the owner, Kazuhiko Kamata, started Gingham in 1981 by opening up a small fashion

Inside /
2K by Gingham

Inside /
page 10

Inside /
Interview

02   03

boutique in Fukuoka, Japan. At the time, there was a high demand for imported fashion items from the US and Europe, so his business was very successful. I joined Gingham and started working with him in 1992. **Is it Gingham or 2K T-shirts? What is the correct name?** This is a timely question. We have recently changed our name to '2K by Gingham' so that 2K by Gingham is now the proper name. **When did you commission your first t-shirt? And what's the story behind it?** I believe that was a series of t-shirts in collaboration with the furniture company Herman Miller Inc. A series of t-shirts with the images of the graphics that were used for their ads in the 50s and 60s. The graphics showed George Nelson and Eames designed furniture. I still love those images, maybe we should re-produce them.

What do you have in mind when you commission a t-shirt? Basically, I either like it or I don't. Other points are: unique or not? New or not new? A motif, a message or a style which reflects today's feeling. When images / designs are offered or catch my eyes, what I often think about is whether 2K by Gingham should be the one introducing those images / artworks to the general public or not. In other words, whether those designs should or could be produced by other people and other companies, and whether it would be better for other companies to do it. Do these images / artworks necessarily have to be introduced by '2K by Gingham'? This is always the question I ask myself. **What kind of artists are you looking for?** An artist who dedicates his / her time and life to create something unique, new and inspiring.

Who do you target with your t-shirts? People who love t-shirts and who love to wear t-shirts. **What age-group and gender?** I would say between 18 to 35 years old. Gender does not matter. **What geographical differences, let's say between Japan, the US and Europe have you experienced when marketing and selling your t-shirts?** The US market is the most conservative. Japan is a totally open, category free market. Once an image / graphic is interesting, they will take it. Europe is also liberal about images / graphics. **Do you get involved in the production process and what is its impact on the result?** Although I do not directly work on it, I supervise my colleagues. Its impact is huge on the result so it is one of the most important parts of our work. **Do you use any special techniques?** Not much. Very few. They are overall prints, combination of direct flocking and ink, combination of foil and silk screening, discharging and enzyme wash. That's about it if you still can call these special techniques. **How many t-shirts do you print of each design?** This totally depends on our customers' orders. Because we produce by orders that are collected by order cut off dates. For some designs, we produce over 3,000 pieces per design per year, and for some designs, we produce only 40 or 50 pieces per design per year. I would say the average would probably be between 150 and 300 pieces per design per year.

Do you think people wear a t-shirt because they agree with the message on the t-shirt or is it just to create a reaction? Both. A t-shirt can be a tool of self-identification and self-expression in urban life. It also can be a tool of communication in urban life. If you wear some of our t-shirts, you will often be addressed to by people you don't even know.

Do you wear t-shirts? Yes. **Tight or loose fit?** Always tight fit. **Long or short sleeve?** Mostly short sleeve. **What makes you buy a t-shirt: the quality, the print, the shape?** Combination of all and the first glance. **Do you wear your own t-shirts?** Yes.

What happens in the winter? We still sell short sleeve t-shirts.

Do t-shirts help designers promoting themselves? Not in general. However, with 2K by Gingham, an artist's name and his / her background information is always provided in hang-tags that are attached to every 2K by Gingham t-shirt, in the catalogues and on the web site. So definitely yes, for the artists who 2K by Gingham work with. **Are t-shirts just a way of getting people to pay for your own advertising?** No. We always would like people to be able to enjoy and have fun by wearing 2K by Gingham.

Do you see evidence of any trends in t-shirt design? Yes. When I see same colours, same motif / theme, same specification of prints and same specification in detail from several different artists. Often, this coincidental overlap happens among design / arts we receive from various artists. So, through the internal daily operations, I see it. But I don't pay much attention to trends in the market. **Do you think the actual trend for wearing t-shirts will end?** The argument as to whether wearing t-shirts is trendy or not does not make sense anymore. It has already become a basic item of urban life. **Or rather, when was the last time you thought that…** Up to three years ago, I thought about it in every summer… **What are your plans for 2K in the future?** Making 2K by Gingham like Levi's in the art t-shirts category. I don't mean a size of business or corporation, but the existence. I mean I would like to turn 2K by Gingham products into very basic items in urban life and in the global urban youth culture network.

What's your favourite t-shirt? And why? In the 2K by Gingham line, this is really a tough question and I cannot name only one as I like all of them. I would say I favour the ones which suit my style and appearance. Beside 2K by Gingham, I love t-shirts that I bought in Maui, as Maui is my favourite place and I visit there every year. Those t-shirts are very local, low key, low resolution in printing and finishing and hand drawings. T-shirts of local surfboard shapers, local fish markets, t-shirts of Slack Key Guitar Music festivals, etc. This is totally personal. By the way, I love tropical islands.

* * *

www.2ktshirts.com

Inside /
2K by Gingham

Inside /
page 11

Inside /
Interview

T-Shirt Survey Part Two

01

01
T-shirt (Aphrodisiac 009)
by MilliMetreKiloLitre

02
Girl Kicking
by Rachel Cattle

03
Stripey Girl
by Rachel Cattle

03
Lost Rabbit
by Darren Watkins /
OKAY OK

T-SHIRT SURVEY

Designers interviewed are (in order of appearance): Experimental Jetset, Darren Watkins / OKAY OK, Michael Place / BUILD, Rachel Cattle, Rockwell, Louise Nowell and MMKL / MilliMetreKiloLitre

QUESTION: Why t-shirts? Why a t-shirt and not a poster?

DARREN WATKINS: This is the most difficult question. I think it's because t-shirts are more appealing and accessible than posters. If you think about making money from t-shirts, which I do, then you'd never sell the same quantities of posters because they hold a different kind of value. T-shirts fade and change shape over time so you can become attached to them. And they hold memories, and when you lend them to someone special you get their smell on it. These are all things I like. Posters just aren't the same.

RACHEL CATTLE: I like the idea of people walking around wearing my drawings. Wearing a drawing seems to change it. It sort of becomes part of the person and the drawings look very different depending on who is wearing them. A poster is a very different thing I think.

MICHAEL PLACE: More exposure. More people seeing you in a cool shirt. Says more about the person. It says I belong.

LOUISE NOWELL: I use the t-shirt as a vehicle to promote my illustrations, being quicker and cheaper than producing work for a poster. In a way t-shirts are more necessary to us than posters, in terms of not being naked.

MilliMetreKiloLitre: It can be a poster, but you would look stupid if you wore a poster! A t-shirt is not just a poster with two sleeves. Everyone needs to wear something and a t-shirt is exactly that in its simplest form. The next step is whether you want to wear just clothes or statements. We are not fashion or clothing designers who make people look good, we are only making statements people can wear and feel good about.

QUESTION When did you design your first t-shirt? And what's the story behind it?

EXPERIMENTAL JETSET: The first proper t-shirt we designed as Experimental Jetset was the 'Black Metal Machine' t-shirt (1998) that we produced as part of an installation piece we did for this great exhibition space called Bureau Amsterdam. The print on the shirt shows a self-portrait of our three faces covered with so-called 'corpse-paint', typical black metal make-up. A few years later we re-released the shirt through 2K by Gingham. Another t-shirt we designed around that same time was the 'My mother went to Amsterdam and all she bought me was this lousy Subliminal shirt' that we designed for Amsterdam skateboard store Subliminal.

DARREN WATKINS: When I moved back to Cardiff in '99, I started a label with two guys that run a great menswear shop called Drooghi. They had the contacts and dealt with business and I designed. We made t-shirts with women's legs printed across them like they were lounging over your chest, and basic shapes in tints. Kinda sharp, classic looking things. It was good, we sold them all over the UK and Japan. They still run it, but now I do my own label (OKAY OK).

RACHEL CATTLE: I had been doing lots of drawings of girls. Mostly images of me or my family from when we were little, mixed with imaginary creatures that I remembered from stories. I liked the idea of printing them onto t-shirts just to see how they would look. My friends Kathy and Brian at Camberwell where we teach helped me get screens made and everything. It was just an experiment to start with.

MICHAEL PLACE: Can't remember. I've lost count.

ROCKWELL: Went to Kinko's or someplace where they do these iron-on t-shirts and made a shirt for Kale-B, a friend of mine…He always used to say 'blij dat ik even zit' so I had that printed on a black tee with white text.

LOUISE NOWELL: My first t-shirt was designed about a year and

02   03

Inside /
Experimental Jetset et al

Inside /
page 12

Inside /
Survey

a half ago, and had an underlying theme based around physical movement and transportation.

MilliMetre: I designed my first t-shirt when I was around seven, I drew a tropical bird on my white t-shirt. A tropical bird was something that I always wanted to see when I was young. I remember I used to wear it a lot and I felt good about it. I still have that t-shirt and it is a good part of my memories. For our t-shirt label, T-Book, we started our 1st t-shirt…umm…with a 'Crush' poem.

KiloLitre: Actually, I remembered when I first got to London I wanted to make a book, and you wanted to make t-shirts. So we agreed to combine the two together. Then you disappeared to Mexico. And one day, you emailed me this Crush poem and it brightened up my day.

QUESTION: Do you work with other labels/companies?

EXPERIMENTAL JETSET: Almost exclusively; we're a graphic design studio, not a t-shirt label. We enjoy working with clients. The only t-shirt we ever put out ourselves was the 'Black Metal Machine' t-shirt, all the other shirts were designed for others. Companies and labels we designed t-shirts for include, among others, 2K by Gingham (Japan), GAS (Japan), So by Alexander van Slobbe (NL) and SoGenes (NL).

DAREEN WATKINS: Not really, just my stockists.

RACHEL CATTLE: I haven't so far. Early on I sent some tees to show Silas and they really liked them and were very encouraging. I'm a big fan so that was a big boost.

MICHAEL PLACE: Yes. Idn, 2K by Gingham, etc.

LOUISE NOWELL: Yes, I'm currently involved with Topshop Boutique combining my prints with a selection of their garments. I've also collaborated with other independent fashion designers and have recently finished work with a group of furniture designers where my images have been used on coffee tables. Working with other areas of design has been hugely enjoyable and an excellent experience, allowing my work to develop in other ways than just a 2-D image. I'm very keen to continue working with other design disciplines.

MilliMetreKiloLitre: Yeah, with a Japanese company we created another label called PROSIT. We did some exhibitions with Levi's, at CINCH London and NIM Paris.

QUESTION: What do you have in mind when you design a t-shirt?

EXPERIMENTAL JETSET: We always try to design a print that underlines the material dimension of the shirt, by making it refer to itself, or to its own context. (That doesn't necessarily mean we always succeed in this.)

DARREN WATKINS: I think about trying to make something I would like wearing myself. And I think about making something timeless, definitive and memorable.

RACHEL CATTLE: I have me in mind pretty much and then just hope other people will like them.

ROCKWELL: Can be a million things, but mostly a reaction to something I saw somewhere…

QUESTION: Who do you target with your t-shirts?
What age-group and gender?

EXPERIMENTAL JETSET: We don't believe in the concept of target audiences at all. Instead of trying to reflect or represent the tastes and lifestyles of presumed target audiences, we rather focus on the inner-logic of the design itself. That way we hope to design objects that relate to society in a healthy, dialectical way. It's a way of designing we notice some people find problematic. Design is often thought of as something that should be experienced by subjects – understood as intuitive human beings – and here we are, talking about design without a subject, trying to focus primarily on the object. It's a form of dialectical materialism some might find really user-unfriendly; but we think it's far from that. How we see it, it's making people happy by not giving them what they want.

DARREN WATKINS: Lawyers, PR executives, tv actors, rock stars, video editors, buyers, grandmothers, rastas, scientists, babies and gardeners.

RACHEL CATTLE: I decided I was just going to do girls for girls at first. Selfish! Then I did some hairy monsters for boys, but boys seem to want to wear the girls more and more so I'm doing some for them too. I guess most people who wear them are my age or younger. No, I'm not telling.

MICHAEL PLACE: Your average Magma browser :)

ROCKWELL: No target…There is no such thing.

LOUISE NOWELL: Essentially I target people like myself (twenties and thirties) but if it appeals to a wider group then that's great. I want to appeal to people who don't necessarily want to be identified with anything in particular other than its specific aesthetic.

MilliMetre: Woo…We hope we can make connections with people who love what we think and what we do. So we are open to whoever loves our t-shirts.

KiloLitre: Well, our t-shirts are all about love and emotions, so I guess anyone who is in love with life.

QUESTION: Do you get involved in the production process and what is its impact on the result?

DARREN WATKINS: My screenprinter's a cool guy so I like working with him.

RACHEL CATTLE: I am the production process. I print them all by hand and sew in all the labels. It's very labour intensive but means I can do as many or few as I want and play with colours more as I go along, which I like.

MICHAEL PLACE: I always get final approval on print/shirt. It matters a lot.

ROCKWELL: I try not to because the printers usually know what they are doing if you give them very strict guidelines.

LOUISE NOWELL: Yes, I'm completely involved. Being in charge of designing and printing each design gives me more control over all aspects as well as saving on money. Ideally it would be good to spend more time on designing and experimenting with new printing techniques and outsource the production process, but that will come.

MilliMetreKiloLitre: We are very, very involved in the whole production process. That's the difference between just putting something on a t-shirt or producing a good quality garment. We want people to feel comfortable when they wear our t-shirts. That means what they wear on the outside and what they feel

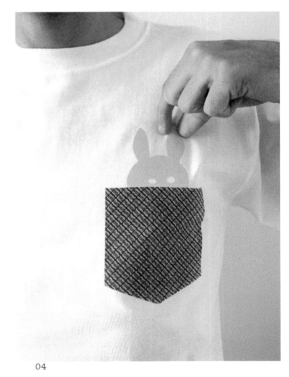

04

Inside/
OKAY OK et al

Inside/
page 13

Inside/
Survey

about the quality. We go through the whole production process and we actually learn a lot about what we can do and what we cannot do. Hence we expand our limits a lot more in our designs. Also we've learnt to communicate with people in different fields who are not necessarily sharing the same language that we use in our design terms.

QUESTION: Do you use any special techniques?
DARREN WATKINS: Not really. I make every print by hand, but is that special?
RACHEL CATTLE: No, just hard labour.
MilliMetreKiloLitre: We are trying every technique that we can find and can't find in the production house. Stuff like flocking and enzyme washes, we need our factory to make them. But if it's something absurd like tie dyeing or weird stitching, we just make them up ourselves. It's good fun. There was one time we had this wicked idea of renewing hypercolour prints. It took us one month to find the right binder!

QUESTION: When you design it do you think of a t-shirt as just an A2 poster or as a moving three-dimensional piece?
EXPERIMENTAL JETSET: 'T-shirtness' is next to 'posterness', but they are still two completely different spheres. Although it should be noted that we see posters also as three-dimensional pieces. And you could argue whether a poster is absolutely immobile, as you suggest; it certainly has a dynamic of its own.
DARREN WATKINS: Some prints I've made would only work on t-shirts. Like a rabbit popping out of a breast pocket. It wouldn't work printed on a piece of paper. Or 'Je Suis La Mascotte de Beauté', so when you wear it you become the mascot of beauty. It's kind of site specific in that it only works when it's worn. So, no, I don't think about it as a poster, only as a t-shirt.
RACHEL CATTLE: I think of it as a drawing first, but then play a lot with the scale and stuff as they look very different on tees than on paper.
MICHAEL PLACE: I think of it as a three-dimensional space that is prone to shrinkage and fading.
LOUISE NOWELL: The placement of the design is very important in terms of it working with your body.
MilliMetreKiloLitre: Well it is 4-D if we really think about it. A t-shirt that will be worn a lot once it is made.

QUESTION: Is mass-production part of the appeal?
EXPERIMENTAL JETSET: Absolutely. The quantity of the shirts certainly adds an extra dimension to the overall concept. The transformation of quantity into quality (and quality into quantity) is something we're quite interested in.
RACHEL CATTLE: I don't mass-produce. I quite like the fact that each one has been done by me so I kind of still feel like I've drawn them all, although I'm starting to get more fed up with the amount of time it all takes so I might have to rethink.
LOUISE NOWELL: At the moment I rather like the human element in producing my clothes, though I'd be happy to see them adorning considerably more people.
MilliMetreKiloLitre: We think the balance between mass-production and limited edition is.

QUESTION: Do you think a t-shirt can convey a political message?
EXPERIMENTAL JETSET: In our view, it's not the message that makes the shirt political. There might be more political potential in the aesthetic, conceptual or contextual dimension of the shirt. To quote Herbert Marcuse from The Aesthetic Dimension: 'Literature can be called revolutionary in a meaningful sense only with reference to itself, as content having become form. The political potential of art lies only in its own aesthetic dimension (...) In this sense, there may be more subversive potential in the poetry of Baudelaire and Rimbaud than in the didactic plays of Brecht'. Of course, Marcuse is talking about literature, but we think the same might be true of graphic design.

05

Experimental Jetset on the concept being the t-shirt:
'The "Anti." t-shirt is an attempt to create an abstract slogan shirt; "Anti." as the archetypical t-shirt slogan. Through this process of abstraction, Experimental Jetset tries to achieve a sense of hermetic self-reference, in an attempt to get away from the representative side of graphic design. Although the shirt can be seen as quite nihilistic and destructive, the slogan itself is in fact a rather optimistic reference to the dialectical philosophy of Hegel, who stated that every given state (thesis) should be confronted with its opposite (antithesis) in order to reach perfection (synthesis). The "Thesis Antithesis Synthesis" t-shirt further explains this principle.

Just like the "Anti." t-shirt is an attempt to create an archetypical slogan t-shirt, the "John Paul Ringo George" t-shirt is an attempt to design an abstract band t-shirt. An iconic shirt, for an iconic band, using four iconic names. A perfect example of pop-cultural abstraction.

The "Structure"-shirt is a simple graphic homage to structures, systems and grids in general. It illustrates that the structure will always be there, even when destroyed or deconstructed. Modernism glorified, and why not?'

'"T-SHIRTNESS" IS NEXT TO "POSTERNESS", BUT THEY ARE STILL TWO COMPLETELY DIFFERENT SPHERES. ALTHOUGH IT SHOULD BE NOTED THAT WE SEE POSTERS ALSO AS THREE-DIMENSIONAL PIECES'
Experimental Jetset

05
T-shirts by
Experimental Jetset
Clockwise from top left:
'Anti.'; 'Structure';
'John Paul Ringo George';
'Thesis Antithesis Synthesis'

06
Lift Off
by Louise Nowell

Inside /
Build et al

Inside /
page 14

Inside /
Survey

DARREN WATKINS: I don't think it's any different on a t-shirt or a poster. Is it? But I think standing at Oxford Circus with a placard and a loudspeaker would reach more people.
RACHEL CATTLE: Yes. I think Michael Marriot's and Alex Rich's 'Shop Local' is a good one.
QUESTION: Do they say something about the wearer?
How personal are they?
RACHEL CATTLE: I think my t-shirts are pretty personal. They're certainly very personal to me. People I talk to who wear them seem to feel quite strongly about them.
MICHAEL PLACE: I think that it says something about the wearer's attitude. They are like a very large ironable badge.
LOUISE NOWELL: The personal buyer will choose a t-shirt because it connects with a part of his or her personality. T-shirts, like any other garment in your wardrobe, convey who you are.

QUESTION: Tight or loose fit?
DARREN WATKINS: Tight-ish.
RACHEL CATTLE: In between.
MICHAEL PLACE: Loose(-ish).
LOUISE NOWELL: Depends on the whole outfit.
MilliMetreKiloLitre: Just fit.
QUESTION: Long or short sleeve?
DARREN WATKINS: Short.
RACHEL CATTLE: Short sleeve.
MICHAEL PLACE: Both. 20.1: Sometimes at the same time.
LOUISE NOWELL: Short.
MilliMetre: Mostly short, but sometimes long.
KiloLitre: Or three-quarter? Or cut up?

QUESTION: What happens in the winter?
DARREN WATKINS: It rains.
RACHEL CATTLE: Sweatshirts.
MICHAEL PLACE: See above (long vs. short question).

QUESTION: Do t-shirts help designers promoting themselves?
Are t-shirts just a way of getting people to pay for your own advertising?
DARREN WATKINS: Not for me. People like wearing the t-shirts I make. My name isn't inside it so nobody who walks into a shop would know that I made it. I've never had any press about what I'm doing. I always give them to a circle of friends but outside that it's a very anonymous thing I do, a small part of my work.
RACHEL CATTLE: Well I'm not advertising anything. People are just wearing my drawings.
EXPERIMENTAL JETSET: None of our shirts have the name Experimental Jetset printed on the front. Neither on the back. So in our case, the answer is no.
LOUISE NOWELL: Yes, both, completely, it's the best way to get your work out and seen. It's a lot quicker than taking your book around to companies.
MilliMetreKiloLitre: T-shirt is just something we do. We like it and we hope people like it too. We think good products are advertisements themselves.

QUESTION Do you see evidence of any trends in t-shirt design?
LOUISE NOWELL: Using embroidery and sewing to depict an image has been around for years now and seems to be popular at the moment. Yes, themes in the design can become trendy too; e.g. insects, eagles, tattoo imagery.
MilliMetreKiloLitre: We don't really care about that.

QUESTION: Do you think the actual trend for wearing t-shirts will end?
DARREN WATKINS: I sometimes wear t-shirts under a jumper or something. It's such an accessible piece of clothing I can't see its popularity ending.
RACHEL CATTLE: I think we might all get bored soon!
MICHAEL PLACE: I don't think it will ever end. They are a cheap way of dressing better.
LOUISE NOWELL: I don't think they'll ever really go out of

06

fashion. A t-shirt is such a simple and functional way of adorning the human body and yet still can convey so much about the wearer.
MilliLitre: Woo…If people stop wearing underwear, then that will be the death of the t-shirt.
KiloLitre: (laughs) Maybe we should wear leaves.

QUESTION: What's your favourite t-shirt? And why?
EXPERIMENTAL JETSET: The anti-war shirt that Katherine Hamnett wore in 1983 when meeting Thatcher [which read '58% Don't Want Pershing' – ed.]. This might seem a strange choice, considering we just wrote that we don't really think it's necessarily the message that makes a shirt political. But then again, we think that (even in this case) it isn't just the message that makes the shirt political. To us, what makes this shirt political is the sheer size of it. A size that underlines the materiality of the t-shirt, its shirtness. Maybe it's the potential of the t-shirt to bear a slogan that makes the shirt political, not the slogan itself.
DARREN WATKINS: A plain classic underwear t-shirt made by 'Jockey'. I like it because it's soft, simple and fits really well.
RACHEL CATTLE: I've got a lovely Silas bear and a nice Tonite one. I like the Silas one because its weird and nice like lots of their stuff…It's not run of the mill. My girl eating an apple is an old favourite too because it's a drawing of me when I was little and strangely my hair looks the same now as when I was nine. What does that mean?
MICHAEL PLACE: My navy blue 'Helvetica Bold' t-shirt. Because it's mine, and I'm the only person who has one.
ROCKWELL: A shirt which says 'West Side School'. I don't know where it's from, probably an eighties American shirt. Really corny and fresh…
LOUISE NOWELL: I don't have a favourite. I change my mind quite a bit.
MilliMetreKiloLitre: Our new collection always.

* * *

Inside /
MMKL et al

Inside /
page 15

Inside /
Survey

Service Form

interview with
Samia Shakra &
Cordula Hentschel
of Service Form
by Inca Starzinsky

01

Service Form are a newly-formed product & ceramic design company based in Cologne, Germany. Graphic spoke to founders Samia Shakra and Cordula Hentschel about their work to date, and their innovative use of ceramics.

You met at University. Why did you choose to work with each other? Does each of you cover a different area or qualities? We quickly found out that working together is a much more intense and inspiring experience. We also push one another very hard and can go deeper into a theme than a single person could. If one of us is not up to the task, the other one is hopefully there to help out for that moment. Another fact is that working together allows you to take part in certain projects and try out things you would not dare to on your own. For sure, we'd say that working as a team is more effective in its outcomes. Productions and ideas simply multiply. It is not really that each of us covers a certain area, it is more a dynamic switch between various disciplines.

The course you originally started was Product and Jewellery Design. Why did you change courses to Ceramic Design? While studying product and jewellery design in Maastricht we discovered our affinity for the techniques of moulding and casting. We were just fascinated by that simple way of producing small series on our own. Both specializations focused on creating products for interiors and everyday life, and this aim has not changed since switching courses. However, we saw in ceramics the potential to develop the kinds of products we had in mind. We simply wanted to transpose our experience and knowledge of typical modern product design onto a very traditional material that has been established in everyday human culture for hundreds of years. The transformation of ceramics from its classical field is the focal point we formulated in our

design works. Porcelain differs from other everyday objects in its higher value and exclusivity; this special position is worthy of keeping but it should be treated more naturally and with less awe. By expanding the field of use we want to integrate porcelain into situations of modern design where it is irreplaceable and unaffected by newly invented materials and high-end technologies. **All your products are made out of ceramic. What intrigues you the most about this material?** It is not only the production techniques but also the characteristic qualities surrounding porcelain that gives us the impulse to work with it. In terms of tableware the qualities of porcelain have not been achieved by any other material. There is nothing else which is so functional and simple on the one hand yet fine and exclusive on the other. There have been generations before that used dishes in the context of tradition, collecting a dish to treat it as a 'sacred' piece. Maybe it is because of this highly cultivated behaviour that there has not been a change or new development in tableware for a very long time. Additionally, the production techniques for china were already brought to a high quality level hundreds of years ago. It is not our aim to break completely with this tradition – there are a lot of ceramic products that are worth collecting and passing on from generation to generation (unlike humans, porcelain does not get old...). In a sense, we want to transfer some of these old-fashioned meanings into a new context, a new tableware culture. **Your first big project was the 'pipelight'. What was the concept behind it and who is it aimed at?** The vision was to create pictures with light and china. Lithopany, very well-known in former times, was a big inspiration. In lithopany, motifs are worked onto extremely thin porcelain sheets and become visible under certain lighting

Inside /
Service Form

Inside /
page 16

Inside /
Interview

'BY EXPANDING THE
FIELD OF USE WE WANT TO
INTEGRATE PORCELAIN
INTO SITUATIONS OF
MODERN DESIGN WHERE
IT IS IRREPLACEABLE'

Bone china is vitreous and is of a brilliant white, very strong and highly translucent, thus allowing light to pass through as if slightly transparent. **At the moment you are working on a catering dish. Tell me about the concept/brief.** Our main interest in this project is the connection to a specific gastronomic concept, which was developed by 3deluxe for the Cocoon club in Frankfurt which opens in the spring. In the context of a new club culture, the two integrated restaurant areas are defined somewhat unusually. The restaurant zone that this dish is designed for will have beds instead of ordinary furniture for sitting and lounging. The dishes therefore act as tools to enable this new eating behaviour. The intention is to confront people with a new table culture in a sensitive way, so that it will easily be accepted because of its functionality. In contrast to a classical serving and eating situation this dish is aimed for use in a more mobile setting. Therefore, it is necessary to reduce the number of pieces while at the same time achieving a variety of combinations for the different demands of the menu. Form and details make sure that the user can handle the dish easily, it being possible to do away with cutlery and the usual furniture. The pieces can be held with one hand or put down on the knees to eat from. The set consists of one base type of bowl which is executed in four different sizes. Additionally there are two trays into which any of the bowls can be set in a pre-designated position. **How do you balance form and function?** It lies in the potential of good china to connect form and function in a very immediate way. The form of each particular piece of china is influenced directly by the field of application. China is a tool, therefore it has to fulfil ergonomical and technical aspects as well as balance, weight, size and volume. All these guidelines have an influence on its shape. We try to develop a form by taking the functional aspects as a starting point. The task is to design functional pieces without giving them too much of a 'cool' or technical appearance. As far as we are concerned, china can combine those rational aspects with a more organic and sometimes even playful character. **What sort of ambitions do you have for your work? What would be an ideal project for you in the future?** It would be wonderful to keep on working on products made of porcelain and other ceramics, but an ideal project would be any project where we get in touch with people and exciting new visions and have the chance to participate and contribute to it.

conditions. The different intensities of light shining through the relief surface of the porcelain sheet creates a beautiful, almost mystic, three-dimensional effect. The disadvantage of this technique is the comparatively small scale that restricts what can be achieved from a single piece of china.

We looked at the idea of creating pictures with light and china and started playing with it; searching for a system in which these pictures would become changeable and not bound to a certain size anymore. The solution we finally came up with is the pipelight. The image area is composed of a number of porcelain sticks; these are arranged in a grid and held in place by holes in a single outer 'screen' section. The sticks can be pushed in and out. The distance to the light source alters the brightness and colour of the light. The user thus has the possibility of creating pictures with light, such as pictograms, letters or abstract patterns.

The pipelight is a self-standing object but is also interesting in combination as an 'infinite' screen on a wall, for example. The pipelight concept can also be seen as a complex illumination system for public space, and can therefore be applied as a guiding or signage system. **Why did you think that ceramics was the most suitable material for it?** We decided to use bone china due to its transparency and its haptic qualities. People are used to this material, so it should feel natural to the touch on one hand but still be able to surprise on the other; simply because this material is not often used in the context of such a product. Searching for the most suitable kind of ceramics, we ended up at the border of the Czech Republic, meeting a Mr Fisher from the Dibbern Company who was so kind as to give us a hundred kilos of finest bone china. What separates bone china from porcelain, stoneware and earthenware is the fact that the composition of bone china typically includes 45–50% bone ash. Bone china is regarded as the highest quality and most expensive material for tableware.

* * *

www.service-form.de
info@service-form.de

02

01
pipelight

02
Samia Shakra &
Cordula Hentschel

03
dish-one

03

Inside /
Service Form

Inside /
page 17

Inside /
Interview

Cultural Physics

an interview with
John Warwicker (Tomato)
by Mairi Duthie

E/VOLCANOES

DE/ALCHEMY

E/CHALK CLIFFS

SIDE/LIGHT

Swedish Archipelago. 1987
Photograph:
John Warwicker

Inside /
Cultural Physics

Inside /
page 18

Inside /
Interview

Seeing the light

You enter a tunnel in the desert in Arizona and emerge in the vast crater of an extinct volcano. Above, framed by the lip of the 400,000 year-old Roden crater is a giant circle containing a constantly shifting and changing canvas of sky. At night it becomes a natural celestial observatory; the galaxies appear to be scattered across a perfectly vaulted dome. Pinpricks of light from nearby planets and distant galaxies reach you, with light waves that may have travelled for perhaps 3 billion years, or as little as one month. You are taking in a cocktail of light of different vintages, which has come a long, long way. This is not familiar old daylight that has bounced around, conveniently illuminating objects for us, and rendered them with the useful appearance of colour. The photons hitting your retina came direct from a far-distant star. The impact of a change of 'frame' or emphasis is stunning – concentrating the mind in a 'pure' experience of light itself.

John Warwicker told me about Roden Crater, during a couple of lively conversations when we grappled with quite abstract and philosophical notions to do with 'experience' in general and the influence of the environment in particular.

He gave the work by American artist James Turrell as an example of perfect, transcendent experience in which the surroundings are key to the impact on the viewer. Whilst the emphasis on space and light on a grand scale is part of the appeal of this vast installation, JW also has a love for things that emphasise constant change and evolution. However, the real attraction for him is the dizzying mixture of artistic, philosophical and scientific ideas contained in the simply beautiful 'thing'... one which can be enjoyed on a basic level, but may transport you in an unexpected way.

With infectious enthusiasm, JW described this mystic effect as follows: 'When a piece of work is truly good it transcends itself... when it has something which you cannot define, which is beyond it and beyond language itself, it just becomes pure experience, which is pure environment, and is a spiritual thing in the proper sense of the word. It is life affirming, and questioning as well. That's what Turrell does, he questions our perceptions.'

What is important to JW is that the inspired moments touched upon above aren't just a one-off, their influence on us goes deeper. 'The power of good writing, good typography, good anything, is that suddenly you see the world again. If you've recognised this transcendent quality... you carry it with you and re-see, rediscover your surroundings.'

These observations are characteristically complex, as JW draws on a heady combination of ideas and imagery in work across a wide range of media from art installations to advertising. Sometimes this can make it hard to pin down what is actually going on, but he likes it that way.

Science And Magic

October will see the publication of The Floating World, which JW has been working on for 20 years, or perhaps even longer than that, as the book arose from conversations with his Grandfather whilst spending summer holidays on the south coast of England as a child. He was a mathematician whose notebook full of symbols and ciphers inspired a lifelong passion for typography in JW. 'Granddad was thinking about language and description, because that's what equations are. To me, it was like weird abstract poetry... with these magical little symbols that somehow had some meaning.' Playing with symbols and words and modulating the effects they can have in relation to each other has been a rich source of exploration.

Other early inspirations came from this man and the environment in which they made their journeys of discovery together. JW paints a vivid verbal picture of a tweedy and distinguished gentleman who entranced his inquisitive and eager grandson with interesting theories about the nature of the world. Walks on the beach at Rottingdean looking at wave movement

gave perfect context to learning about chaos theory and the way momentum and non-linear forces build the surging patterns of nature. 'You could see what his equations actually meant physically... the fractal self-similarity that happens constantly.'

'My first drawings were made with chalk from the base of the cliffs, and I remember building sculptures... we would also visit the long man at Wilmington – a huge chalk drawing, or cut, in the grass. To a six year old there was a magical connection and a sort of historical continuance between the chalk itself and this really weird old figure, in an extraordinary pose. On a basic level, as a puppy-like kid I thought, "God, that's a big drawing!"'

Blurring Boundaries

Memory, and the interface of the internal and external environment is something JW has worked on capturing in 'mapping' – a process which could be described as tracing different influences and their effects using different languages. One strand to this method is the understanding that you are not able definitively to describe or convey anything exactly; it is always 'coloured' by both the form of language used and the individual 'filters' imposed by yourself in describing, and the viewer in looking.

Another part of this approach is based on a strong conviction that everything (ourselves included) is in a constant state of development and evolution, so nothing is static or fixed. If you take this open-eyed and open-minded view, you are more likely to come up with an unexpected result. 'I try to retain the naivety of a six year old looking at the world, and being in the world, which is very hard.'

So JW's way of working actively encourages the happy accident, the mysterious eureka moment that is as hard to define, as to make happen; 'Sometimes I deliberately collide two different ways of thinking or doing to see what happens... that's alchemy.' He might immerse himself in film titles whilst thinking about an architecture project, for example. 'It's not rocket science, quite simply, that in moving, say, from film to music to sculpture you are stepping outside a given discipline and superimposing a different formal language on the situation.' So from this, a fresh perspective might arise: 'Rather than have a pre-determined end-point, I like to put two, three, any number of things together and see what happens. I'm not a Modernist in the sense of keeping within a certain methodology and working towards a pre-determined aesthetic.'

JW seeks magical uncertainties and indefinable serendipities...

The way in which he encourages these creative quantum leaps is through 'conversation' – something that has been applied in the Tomato creative workshops over the years – where the emphasis is on interaction and the development of ideas known by Tomato as 'process'.

'What people might identify as the 'work' or result, is often the thing which comes out of the real work – which is the conversation. The dynamic between you, the material and the idea, often an internalised dialogue, is the forming

Inside /
Cultural Physics

Inside /
page 19

Inside /
Interview

of the 'work'. Working on a film, for example, because you are working with people, the forming of the film is a continuous conversation right up to the point when it gets released into the world.'

Shared Experience

Another art installation / environment we discussed was the transformation of the turbine hall at the Tate Modern by Olafur Eliasson where space and light were used to powerful effect – but which is perhaps more notable for the way people behaved. In a misty atmosphere lit by a giant yellow 'sun', crowds lay on the floor, often starfish-fashion or making shapes in a group, seeing their reflections in a mirrored ceiling high above. In this slightly weird environment, with oddly subdued colour, there was a strong sense of friendly human interaction; a rather expansive feeling predominated. It would have been quite different to be there on your own, I suggested. JW agreed and disagreed, 'What's interesting about those sorts of things is that you do get a sense of community, or gathering, and it works at a more primal level than, say, theatre…However, people go in with their own lives and leave with their own lives…and they don't see [the work] in the same way. The personal experience of each is different. You could say it's a common experience, individually realised.'

Colour

A reddish-brown door encountered on a photoshoot in the Swedish archipelago sounds an unlikely source of a creative outburst. Not for JW, who loved the shade, which he'd never seen before, and set out to find why…'the pigment was made from a local iron ore, so it was unique to the area.'

Horsehead Nebula
JW in Tomato project
at the Museum of
Contemporary Art,
Castellon, Spain. 2002

The abundance and variety of colour 'in real life', and its variation, spurred him to react against the limitations of the Pantone reference, and the colour palette available on the computer screen.

The colour series also came about partly through the impact of the location itself; 'McDonald's yellow, even though it is globally produced to the same colour standard, looks different in London, New York and Tokyo because of the atmospheres and so on…so suddenly I thought about the colour register, a colour code of time and place, the colour of time.'

Another thing the Eliasson piece emphasised in its bleaching-out of colour was the fact that there is, in fact, no inherent colour – it's just bounced light, and, as JW points out, 'light through things…is affected by their material quality. Did you know that light slows down when it goes through a diamond? Light slows down, so time slows down'.

It is strange to think that we may all see colours themselves differently (How would I know if your green was my purple? Only because we've agreed on the name for the colour of grass). JW, however sees colours very differently from most of us, being himself profoundly colour-blind but with extremely acute tonal sight.

It is, furthermore, difficult to imagine how JW manages to manipulate and use colour in sophisticated and subtle ways if he sees almost in monochrome, even when he explains, 'I learned colour academically, or intellectually, which is possibly good because I don't take it for granted. I am always searching for colour and its effect. For example, put a Japanese pink against a Brazilian orange, that's interesting.'

This mixing and matching and eclecticism is a constant in JW's work.

Collective Identity

In a typically lateral response to a brief to create a static logo for Sony networking technologies, Tomato 'asked the most basic and obvious question, which was: What shape is a network? How big is the internet?'

They created a generative motor which uses sensors in the outside world which detect movement, colour, heat, and converts them into algorithms. These affect the behaviour of all the elements of the on-screen identity; altering colours and the speed of the transient shapes…producing an ever-changing 'identity' for Sony, which is not controlled by anyone, but shifts and changes with the different external stimuli. 'It is 'of-the-world' not 'on-the-world' as most logos are.'

People can contribute directly, by choosing a word on the website, which led to the question of whether the identity itself was a collective one, or if such a thing exists…

Cultural Physics

JW's focus on what makes us tick, and how this influences both self-expression and behaviour is, as mentioned before, a blend of scientific inquiry and theory with philosophical and sociological matters, an approach which sometimes 'gets a bit vague', he cheerfully admits. As we spoke, he decided that it was all about 'cultural physics', which seems a good name

'HIS WAY OF WORKING
ACTIVELY ENCOURAGES
THE HAPPY ACCIDENT,
THE MYSTERIOUS
EUREKA MOMENT…'

Inside /
Cultural Physics

Inside /
page 20

Inside /
Interview

for his own particular area of inquiry into 'individual behaviour within the collective.'

'The interesting thing about humans is that the world is bigger than ourselves, and we are taking things in through our senses all the time and interpreting them through our filters. But we can only express ourselves in linear time, through whatever language.' He goes on to elaborate that it is the limitations which make it impossible accurately to convey our actual experience that fascinate him – 'the human condition', which means that symbol and metaphor are the nearest we get to conveying a moment.

We go back to the sea for a moment, as JW talks about the dynamics of social and cultural change. It is a powerful way to illustrate the point that tiny changes, added together and building up, can lead to surges of energy, with ongoing motion and momentum.

'Here we go, Grandad's sea metaphor again…the sea is the sea everywhere. It doesn't suddenly go from calm to storm, but is influenced constantly by climate, winds, undercurrents. In human history revolutions often happen through the accumulation of those tiny things you cannot see…people's minds and attitudes slowly and surely change, often over a long period of time. They then enforce change…often cataclysmically.' JW added that the ebbing and flowing of ideas and views in different times and regions is illustrated by today's simultaneous existence of fundamentalism and modern secular multiculturalism.

'What's so frightening about fundamentalism is its conformity and its certainty of "the right way" which ignores

the fact that there have always been other ways and there always will be.'

Human nature & behaviour are fascinating to JW: 'There are only two cultures, the individual and the world, and then the world is divided up into sub-cultures. The reason we have 'tribes' is partly because we are a social animal, and partly because of uncertainty…at a primal level this uncertainty breeds control and belief.' JW is drawing together the strands of politics, belief systems and the development of ideas in another book project, 'Cultural Physics'. In the meantime, he will be finishing the existing Floating World work-in-progress (with Michael Mack) and still actively participating in Tomato, as well as working on a long-term project as a creative partner at Grey Advertising.

'Whilst I thrive on the more abstract, intellectual projects like these books, at the same time my work in 'the industry' is also satisfying in another way. The design and communications world is an interesting crucible for the creative alchemic process…a little black and white ad can be something beautiful and wonderful in its own right…and one always tries to make it so.'

* * *

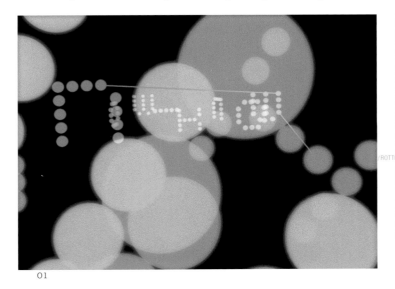

01

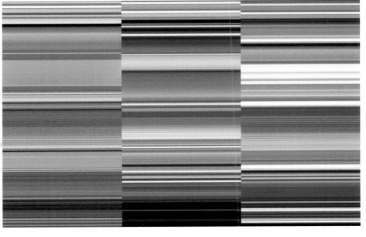

03

02

04

Inside /
Cultural Physics

Inside /
page 21

Inside /
Interview

A Practice For Everyday Life

interview by Lachlan Blackley

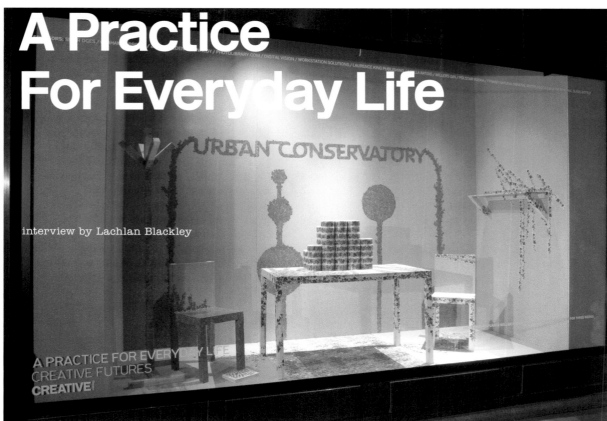

01

Voted Creative Futures 2003 (hosted by Creative Review Magazine), A Practice for Everyday Life is a young London-based design company, formed by Kirsty Carter and Emma Thomas. Incorporating the environment and drawing inspiration from everyday life, their products and projects suggest a subtle humour by highlighting things that tend to go unnoticed. We asked them about their <u>Urban Conservatory</u> and how the <u>Grey Blanket</u> project helped raise awareness of city pollution.

Can you explain further the name of your company <u>A Practice for Everyday Life</u>? We didn't want our company name to be our names. I suppose we liked the idea of being personally anonymous to our projects and choosing a name which represented more what the company does, rather than us, Kirsty Carter and Emma Thomas. We both read and enjoyed a particular book, Michel de Certeau's <u>The Practice of Everyday Life</u> and realised our working process related to it. Everyday life is something that we use as inspiration, from what is often taken for granted. Our work often draws upon everyday ephemera. Our inspiration and we hope our work is located in real life, in the language of the banal, the ordinary and familiar. I suppose we prefer to present things as they are rather than incorporating or submitting them into an overly manufactured design process. **What are your concerns with design and the products that you create?** We don't have a manifesto, I am not sure if we really believe in manifestos. People and design are ever changing. To write those sorts of things down seems somewhat arrogant. What we really are concerned with is that the work we do is thoughtful and custom-made to each project's specific needs. We are concerned with thinking and producing the project's idea in the simplest way and whether it communicates to the people it needs to. Every project we work on is different and requires something different from us each time. That is what makes our life exciting and fills the project with energy. **What are your ideas about changing an environment with your products / projects?** Sometimes we feel our environments could be more pleasant by adding a little humour or highlighting

02

© A Practice for Everyday Life

something that people may miss or walk past without noticing. Slightly altering or adding something could change it altogether, transforming it from a rather boring, suppressive environment into more of a pleasurable, interesting one. **Your Urban Conservatory project brings nature back into an urban environment – can you explain this idea further?** The Urban Conservatory project was about being able to apply a bit of nature indoors, in particular to a flat (home) in the town or city. The city doesn't want to allow us much room to see life grow. Being able to enjoy your own bit of nature – whether a lawn, a scraggy bush, a flowerbed or window box – means a lot. Plants grow, die and are bought again. To save time and money, we created 1:1 scale plant products (stickers, posters, and tape) that we can have and use to change the interior of the home or office. These urban conservatory print products add nature / a bit of greenery to ordinary furniture, walls, doors etc, almost making them alive! **How did the project develop?** We won this year's Creative Futures and we were asked to do a window display at Selfridges Department store of our own work. The Urban Conservatory project was inspired and developed by a comment made by the

Inside /
A Practice For Everyday Life

Inside /
page 22

Inside /
Interview

WE WANTED TO TRANSFORM
A PUBLIC SPACE TO RAISE
AWARENESS OF WHAT PEOPLE
TAKE FOR GRANTED
AND TO DISRUPT THE GREY
MONOTONOUS ROUTINE
OF OUR CITY

Selfridges window display team – they told us 'Don't use anything that can not stand the heat, even in winter the windows get very hot, it's like a conservatory'. We really liked this idea of it being a conservatory right in the middle of Oxford Street, so we took them literally. If we had just made it a real conservatory though, the project could not go beyond Selfridges. People find real plants hard to grow – always too busy to remember to water them. So we decided to use the production budget to create printed matter plants. **How do people respond to your products?** They think they're great, people use them just as we hoped – in all sorts of ways. The Ivy tape for example we used to hold some furniture we built for our studio. Emma's mum used hers on her Christmas wrapping paper. However people choose to use it, it lets that plant grow and makes it more of an interesting, pleasurable object or place to be.

How did the idea come about for the Grey Blanket project? The idea for the Grey Blanket came from numerous ideas, projects and discussions we had and specifically a few projects we did before the Grey Blanket. We were cycling across central London every day and were conscious of how polluted the city was. The project just accelerated from there – discussions about white vans with 'clean me' on, to Duchamp's Dust built-up on the Large Glass. And an extract from a book we were reading called 'Fragments of the European City' by Stephen Barber. '… so that the faces incorporate the city as a surface of lines, textures, marks, scars. The dirt of the city rapidly builds upon the surface skin of the city's inhabitants, and any face caught in static in the street will be encrusted with the expulsive languages of the city as pervasively as is the surface of the city's buildings.'

We began to be more aware of what the city would actually look like when you cleaned the grey dirt off the surfaces of all the buildings. We wanted to transform a public space to raise awareness of what people take for granted and to disrupt the grey monotonous routine of our city. We were aware we were not defacing, damaging or harming the city, only using the urban process of pollution, to draw attention to itself as though the city itself created the works.

'4m long typographic messages, rubbed out of pollution build-up, raise awareness of what we breath in everyday, on every journey around London. Created by cleaning off areas of carbon emissions built up on surfaces around the city, they reveal buildings, walls, and tiles which have been hidden for years under the grey blanket of pollution. Find them across London from Hyde Park Corner underpass to Tower Bridge Road, before the city is completely cleaned up, or enough pollutants build up again for the message to vanish.' – Our press release

What response did you get back? Did it raise awareness do you think? The best thing about doing this project (something we never anticipated), is we actually got the council into action and they began to clean the buildings, underpasses and walls we had been rubbing away at. It did stop the public seeing the message, but that didn't matter because it meant we were actually making a difference. We created an awareness which directly got the councils to clean their borough, which has in a small way helped London to be a better, more pleasurable place to live in. Once they had seen our (clean) graffiti, they had to clean it off. The ones they did leave, the public would see and be more aware of what they are breathing and what lies beneath London's buildings.

*   *   *

www.apracticeforeverydaylife.com

03

04

Inside /
A Practice For Everyday Life

Inside /
page 23

Inside /
Interview

Hello, my name is ...

interview with
Chad Rea (86 the onions)
by Lachlan Blackley

01

Inside /
86 the onions

Inside /
page 24

Inside /
Interview

02

With a disappointing lack of interest and support from local charity organisations, L.A. based creative director and writer, Chad Rea, appealed to photographers around the world to help create an awareness of the homeless problem in our communities. By distributing giant name tags and asking the homeless to write their own name, the Hello My Name Is ... project aims to help the homeless feel they have an identity within the community – to be recognised not as street trash, but as individual human beings with a name.

What inspired you to begin this project? There are a lot of homeless people in Venice, California. I walk past one guy in particular to and from work every day. It wasn't until I learned his name, Robertson, that I stopped looking at him as a panhandler, but a person that I wanted to know more about and help. I wondered if my experience could work on a larger scale. **What was the basic idea behind it?** Originally, the idea was to distribute 5,000 of these giant nametags to the homeless in Los Angeles over the course of one weekend. I thought it was be great if the homeless started a movement or a sort of uprising and every street corner was occupied by a homeless person holding up a sign, demanding that they be seen as human beings and not trash. I wanted the homeless issue to be front-page news, simply build awareness by giving the homeless a voice, and give homeless organisations a platform to offer solutions.

How did this develop? After months of mostly positive meetings with local homeless organisations to help with the distributions of signs, a unified effort proved to be impossible due to religious, political, or selfish motivations. Rather than let

01
Bruce
photographed by
Stijn & Marie-José

02
Yacub
photographed by
Jay Newman

'I THOUGHT IT WOULD BE GREAT IF THE HOMELESS STARTED A MOVEMENT OR A SORT OF UPRISING AND EVERY STREET CORNER WAS OCCUPIED BY A HOMELESS PERSON HOLDING UP A SIGN, DEMANDING THAT THEY BE SEEN AS HUMAN BEINGS AND NOT TRASH'

the idea die, we thought the idea could even have more impact if we distributed them to photographers around the world and let them photograph homeless people in their community. We will compile the images for a website, an exhibition, and a book. But it's encouraged that everyone involved to push it even further. If they want to have their own local exhibition, start their own movement, whatever, great.

I would like to point out that our logo is nowhere on the signs. This is not a PR stunt or a way to say, 'Aren't 86 the onions good people?'. So many corporations donate money for selfish reasons. We are not one of those people. We are simply using our creative talents to get a positive message out to the public. It is a random act of kindness that we hope others are inspired by and do something similar.

Inside /
86 the onions

Inside /
page 25

Inside /
Interview

03

03
Ma Boo
photographed by
Pete Vattanatham

04
Ruth
photographed by
Lenard Smith

04

'WE TOUCHED ON SOMETHING MANY FIND ONE OF THE MOST DIFFICULT THINGS ABOUT LIVING ON THE STREET – NEVER HEARING YOUR NAME'

What are your thoughts on name/identity and this distance we have with the homeless? Well, based on my own experience, it makes you see homelessness in a new light, with respect. And from the meetings I had with homeless people and homeless organisations run by ex-homeless people, we touched on something many find one of the most difficult things about living on the street – never hearing your name.

What help or challenges did you face from charity organisations in trying to set this up? It was an interesting experience. There were some organisations that just weren't interested for whatever reason. We did find one local mission who had recently been gathering with other missions a few times a year. I was able to present to all of these organisations. Everyone loved the idea. One man cried. Many suggested other ways to use the idea, like at their dignity parade last November. To display the signs on their wall or to give them to the three hundred homeless people who meet with City Council once a month. No one ever returned my calls or emails from that point forward. The only negative

OUTSIDE/BRUCE

OUTSIDE/BARBARA

OUTSIDE/HOSEA

05

things I heard was that it encouraged panhandling and that some people actually wanted to remain anonymous. **How do you think this will be different from the usual charity project? How will it grab people's attention and raise awareness?** It's selfless; a random act of kindness. It doesn't require a lot of energy to get involved. It's more personal. It deals with individuals as opposed to an entire group; it's one on one. It doesn't use traditional media or the typical visual or written language of charity. It doesn't make you feel guilty. It's not asking for money, just your respect. It gives individuals a voice instead of letting an organisation speak for them. It has the potential to spread globally with very little effort. **In what way do you think this project will contribute towards solving or easing the homeless problem?** If anything, I hope it will bring attention to the homeless issue. Hopefully, it touches people enough to want to get involved, help spread the word, volunteer, donate time / money, write to their senator or city council member, etc. It's not going to solve the problem, but maybe it'll grow into something that can cause change. If it gets one person off the streets and their life back on track,

then it's been successful. **How did the homeless react to being a part of this?** Depends. I've heard, 'This is exactly how I'm feeling today. Thank you'. And I've heard of photographers running into people who don't want to be bothered, or known. Some are mentally ill. I've heard from one person that they get more money because of the sign.

Why did you get photographers involved? We thought seeing 5,000 images of homeless people from all corners of the globe would be really powerful. It made it both a global and local issue. It made it more newsworthy – instead of just being about Los Angeles. **What has the response been like from photographers?** So far so good. A few people have found some homeless people to be quite difficult and only sent in one picture instead of 10. Others have asked for 50 signs. Signs are being mailed out daily. So far, we've distributed over 3,500 signs in 22 U.S. states and 13 countries. **Did you approach 'name' photographers?** The majority if not all are professionals. Some have 'names' but we're not that knowledgeable of who's who, especially when the brief's gone

Inside /
86 the onions

Inside /
page 27

Inside /
Interview

06

Inside /
86 the onions

Inside /
page 28

Inside /
Interview

06
Ingo
photographed by
Stijn & Marie-José

07
Glichless
photographed by
Michael Bowles

OUTSIDE/VISIBILITY

OUTSIDE/PERSONALITY

OUTSIDE/DIGNITY

07

around the world. (Know any? I think it would help get others involved.) We've asked for samples of everyone's work and they are all extremely capable and talented. We haven't turned anyone down and plan on using everyone's contributions. All we've asked is that the homeless person write their own name and hold the sign. Everything else is up to the photographer, and with so many different specialist we hope each photograph is very different.

What ideas do you have for using the media with this project? Has the media helped in any way? The creative trade press has been pretty good. Brandweek, Creativity (both US), Addict magazine (Belgium), Marmalade (UK), IDANDA.net (US) and possibly Los Angeles magazine have or are going to do a piece on the project. I have also been invited to speak at this years Clio Awards about the project. While we've emailed USA Today, The Washington Post, The LA Times, and The NY Times, among others (Oprah), we've gotten no response. **Has this project inspired new ideas?** So far, we've been asked for the artwork by two companies who will make more signs and their own projects. We've recently been contacted by a photography grad student who wants to do her thesis on the project. And we're currently working with a director to bring the idea to motion picture. We're also reaching toward

starting a foundation to help fund future projects benefiting the homeless.

Nelson Cabrera, a commercial film director, is shooting ten 15-second PSAs – each featuring one homeless person in their environment, holding the signs, saying things like: 'What do you call someone who lives on the street?' and 'We have a lot more in common than you thnk'. And 'Out of all the names you could call me, try one I rarely hear'. Each commercial ends with 'www.projecthello.org'.

When do you hope a book will be published with this work? At this rate, end of the year. Maybe in time for National Homeless Day, which is in November. **What's the closing date for photographers wanting to contribute to this project?** The deadline for photographers interested in this project is May 1st 2004.

* * *

info@86theonions.com
www.projecthello.org

OUTSIDE/STREETS

OUTSIDE/IDENTITY

Inside /
86 the onions

Inside /
page 29

Inside /
Interview

Marc Craste

interview by Lachlan Blackley

STUDIOAKA
PRESENTS

A FILM BY MARC CRASTE

JOJO in the STARS

STUDIOAKA PRESENTS A FILM BY MARC CRASTE JO JO IN THE STARS MUSIC BY DIE KNÖDEL DUMB TYPE SAMUEL BARBER SOUND DESIGNER HILARY WYATT
FEATURING THE VOICE OF OLIVER MICELI AS MDME PICA CG ARTISTS FABRICE ALTMAN DUNCAN BURCH JAMES GAILLARD
DOMINIC GRIFFITHS TALIA HILL BORIS KOSSMEHL FABIENNE RIVORY JAMES ROGERS ANDY STAVELEY BRAM TTWHEAM
EDITED BY WILLIAM EAGAR PRODUCTION ASSISTANTS LINDSEY FRAINE REN PESCI TRACEY ASHFORD EXECUTIVE PRODUCERS PAM DENNIS SUE GOFFE PHILIP HUNT
DOLBY DIGITAL IN SELECTED THEATRES PRODUCED BY SUE GOFFE WRITTEN DESIGNED AND DIRECTED BY MARC CRASTE

© MMIII STUDIOaka ALL RIGHTS RESERVED

01

**Inside /
Marc Craste**

**Inside /
page 30**

**Inside /
Interview**

> 'THERE'S SOMETHING ABOUT PEOPLE BEING DWARFED BY THEIR SURROUNDINGS. IT'S THE SETTING THAT'S THE REAL CHARACTER OF THE FILM WITH THESE SORT OF VAST BUILDINGS, TINY CHARACTERS AND GREAT BIG DOORS …'

With a successful portfolio of 30 second commercials (including Natwest, Orange and Compaq Web), animation director, Marc Craste, of Studio AKA in London, has written and directed his first short film. Created in CG, <u>Jo Jo in the Stars</u> is the dark and beautiful love story of two strange characters trapped in the bleak setting of Madam Pica's freak show. Produced by Studio AKA, the film was nominated and picked up best animation short at this year's BAFTA awards [just as we went to print]. Marc discusses the inspiration of music in his work, his influences and obsession with freak shows.

How did you start the idea for this film?
About 4 or 5 years ago I did a pitch for Channel Four and I came up with these little characters called picas. Then we made three little films called Pica Towers, which we put on the web site and got a good response from people. And it was just sort of an extension of that – just trying to actually do something with the story because Pica Towers had no story what so ever. I suggested a little 6min film to the studio and it turned out to be 12min.

What inspired the 'look' of your characters?
Mainly for pragmatic reasons, everything was supposed to be inexpensive and done as quickly as possible. As far as characters go that you make in CG – they're just little bean shapes with little sausage legs and arms – you can't really get much simpler than that. Originally they had little TV aerials which was tied into the idea for Channel Four and I got rid of those and gave them rabbit ears instead. And with all the freaks that you see in the freak show, the idea was again for practical reasons, just to make masks that fit over a standard pica character. I have this book on Upick masks, which are fabulous masks that have these sort of cartoony grotesque faces. So there's a little bit of that thrown in.

It's very cinematic – were you influenced by films like Citizen Kane and Metropolis with the big scale buildings and oppressive environments?
When I did this film I started seeing a common thread throughout … not only in this, but even some of the commercials I did. The way that I lay them out you tend to get the character down in the bottom right hand corner in this vast set. So there's something about people being dwarfed by their surroundings. It's the setting that's the real character of the film with these sort of vast buildings, tiny characters and great big doors with handles that are way too big for them to open. But trying to pick influences on this, a couple of people have said Citizen Kane. And Metropolis has come up. I think Brazil is influential. I remember when it first came out I loved it. That whole thing of the buildings coming up through the ground and him being stuck inside it. And I think Eraserhead as well – that sort of lonesome figure walking against a great big industrial site … so all those things have sort of come out.

Do you have direct influences with your work?
I don't think so. I've only ever really thought about it in the last few months as people have been asking me and because I'm not good at collecting things or remembering things or putting names to things – my knowledge of films is pathetically weak. I'm forever sitting in meetings where people will mention something and I'll nod knowingly … but I just don't have a clue. And I think it's just an amalgamation over the years. I'm sure every time I see something a little bit seeps in and you just pick the bits that you like. But I'm hopeless at cataloguing it and then saying this person was a direct influence or not. There's definitely the whole freak show thing. Todd Browning's Freaks had a huge impact when I was young. It's a 1930s black and white film, which actually featured real freaks and it was incredibly atmospheric. So from that to side show music, which I really like, there's this 15–20 year obsession and I'm not entirely sure why.

What sparks your imagination?
The music in this – the bit when she's on the trapeze and the bit in the end – is by an Austrian folk band called <u>die Knodel</u>. I'd heard it in the studio one day and I thought 'That is just the most melancholic beautiful bit of music'. I played it to death until I got sick of it and then with this ongoing obsession with circuses and whatever, it just sort of came together. I thought it would be just fabulous music to have something really sad happening to. And that really was the inspiration for the whole film.

How do you come up with your ideas?
Prior to doing this film there were people saying 'Are you gonna make a film?' And I was like 'Yeah I'd love to make a film but I'm completely bereft of ideas and nothing ever gels as an idea'. And what it sort of taught me is that it's not such a bad thing to just

01
Jojo In The Stars
Poster

02
Jojo In The Stars
Film Still

02

Inside /
Marc Craste

Inside /
page 31

Inside /
Interview

keep having the characters and writing down ideas – just having all that in a drawer and waiting for the moment when two things can gel rather than have nothing to go with. In a way it was such an easy process from 'I think I'll make a film about a circus featuring these characters with this bit of music'. The storyboard, the rough storyboarding was like you know, a day's work to go through… I just went 'I'll have this, this, this and this' and went blurgh! And although a lot got tweaked in the process of making it, I think it was sort of meant to be as far as that was concerned.

Is there a message that you're trying to get across in this film?

Yeah I think there is… It depends because people interpret it in different ways and I quite like the fact that some people see it as a happy ending and some people see it as a sad ending. Basically it's 'inappropriate love' – falling in love with the wrong person at the wrong time, what you'll risk for it and the price you may pay for risking that. And then at the end it's like, well is it that love triumphs or prevails and you make the best of what the world throws at you? In effect, they're forever separated by these bars, but that's better than one being inside the building and one out. And people say to me, the reason it works is that it's so tongue in cheek. But I'm not entirely sure it is that tongue in cheek. What I wanted to do was take ridiculous looking characters and a ridiculous set and then try and tell something which really is honestly about the whole romance and how a little person gets courage when he goes to rescue her. So it's actually quite sort of heart on the sleeve. But if people want to take it as tongue in cheek…

I think that's why it turned out visually as beautiful as it did. Originally when the two of them get together we had this sort of comic romp. We thought wouldn't it be hilarious to see what it's like to have two Picas shagging because they keep rolling off each other. And then Pam, the managing director, kept saying to me 'Just remember what you were trying to make here. Don't get sidetracked into doing these little comic things'. And then it went back to yeah, maybe it's nice with clouds and tinfoil stars and everything which is originally what it was suppose to be – just drop-dead gorgeous with these sort of grand themes.

Do you have a new project that you would like to put into production?

There's one other project, which I'm trying to get through now. We're doing a 3min trailer to try to sell a script idea. I've got a much bigger version of Picas which is a feature length thing called <u>Tower of Blood</u>. But nothing else really concrete. But I'm not as panicked about that as I used to be. I think it's not until you make something and given that I started this in my mid to late 30s – that's a long time between the age of 20 saying 'I want to make a film' to actually starting to make a film. You begin to think, you know, maybe all the technical know-how is there but there's nothing to say. And then all of a sudden the forces come together serendipitously. It's gotta be a lot of hard graft as well and hard work but it can be pure coincidence and luck that sets you off on a path.

What made you decide to do animation?

I went to see Fantasia when I was about six and you know, Night On Bald Mountain? I came home and tried to do a drawing of

03

Inside /
Marc Craste

Inside /
page 32

Inside /
Interview

04

05

'WHAT I WANTED TO DO
WAS TAKE RIDICULOUS LOOKING
CHARACTERS AND A
RIDICULOUS SET
AND THEN TRY AND TELL
SOMETHING WHICH REALLY
IS HONESTLY ABOUT THE
WHOLE ROMANCE AND
HOW A LITTLE PERSON GETS
COURAGE WHEN HE GOES TO
RESCUE HER.'

06

03
Jojo In The Stars
'Mural'

04–06
Jojo In The Stars
Film Stills

Inside /
Marc Craste

Inside /
page 33

Inside /
Interview

01,02
Jojo In The Stars
Film Stills

01

02

OUTSIDE/TODD BROWNING

OUTSIDE/DIE KNODEL   OUTSIDE/METROPOLIS   OUTSIDE/BUILDINGS

the devil on top of the mountain with big bat wings. And I remember at the time I couldn't work out how they'd done his legs because what I didn't pick up in the film was that he was actually part of the mountain. And I still have that drawing – this hilarious drawing of this big bubbly muscley body with bat wings and these little spindly legs. **Like your characters ...** Exactly! I was just so blown away by that film and I knew it was all drawings and that's what knocked me out – the skill to bring that to life and everything. So it was just an obsession from that point onwards until I actually sat down to do it and realised how difficult it was and thought 'Oh ...'

Where did you train?
I didn't, I just left school. I was in Sydney when I started working. I just went and knocked on the doors of animation studios with my portfolio of little crumpled bits of paper and got a job doing TV Saturday morning animation. And then somebody came over from London whom I met socially. They were looking to start a commercial studio and said to me 'If you want to learn how to do good animation you've gotta do it in commercials because it doesn't happen in TV stuff'. So I went with them for a while and just stayed in commercials from then on. And then I came to London and this was the first place I walked into. **Studio AKA?** Yeah. I just happened to walk in the day they needed a character to be designed quickly and I've been here 7 or 8 years now. My only intention coming to London was to walk away with a good showreel of commercials so I've sort of got that and now I've got a film.

So where will it be shown?
We'll have our showing for the crew and the cast of one and industry people. Beyond that it's putting it into festivals and seeing if it gets a good response there. And after that I don't know. I don't know, what you do with a 12min film? **Can you see it being shown before a feature?** Yeah, ideally it would be somebody picking it up. You know, I thought it was a shame prior to having made a film and now I've got this film I think it's insane that they don't do that. I would have thought attached to the right sort of film ... I mean if there were a re-run of Wings of Desire it would fit with that. Eraserhead it would fit with. Or Tim Burton's new stop motion film.

Would you like to direct a longer animated feature?
Yeah I'd love to now. And in a way I feel like this has been my big self-indulgent rant, which I've done. I'd be extremely happy if somebody walked in with a script that was sort of something I liked. Then I could bring all that I would bring to a commercial script and bring that to the story. I don't feel the need for it to be my own story, but I s'pose you bring so much to it anyway. I think I'd prefer that at the moment.

*   *   *

www.studioaka.com

OUTSIDE/WALT DISNEY   OUTSIDE/BALD MOUNTAIN   OUTSIDE/DRAWINGS

**Inside /
Marc Craste**

**Inside /
page 34**

**Inside /
Interview**

The Designers Republic Book
A Brief History

interview with Ian Anderson
of The Designers Republic on their
forever-forthcoming book.
by Marc-A Valli

'Excuse me, do you know when the Designers Republic book is coming out?'

I had just started working for this bookshop on Charing X road and this was one of the first questions a customer ever asked me. I told the customer that I didn't know and enquired as to whether he had actually heard of such book being announced. He assured me that he had, that its publication was imminent. So I looked for it into our Books-In-Print database and yes, the title was there, along with a publisher's name and a price – all that was missing was a publication date … I expressed my frustration with the database and suggested that the customer come back for it the following week. The same scene repeated itself again and again until someone in the bookshop decided to call TDR to ask them the question directly. Someone at TDR assured him that, yes, the book would be coming out, but that they didn't know exactly when.

That was eight years ago. A lot happened since. I left that job to start another bookshop along with a colleague, the publisher mentioned in the database went into receivership and so did the bookshop we used to worked for … But not a week goes by without a customer walking into our shop (I sometimes wonder whether we will still be in business by the time the book comes out) and asking, 'Excuse me, do you know when the Designers Republic book is …'

Don't. Just don't ask.

Marc Valli

So, when is it coming out? Soon. 2004. **When did you first think about doing a Designers Republic book?** When (publisher) Edward Booth Clibborn offered us a king's ransom in 1994. **Has the idea of the book changed a lot since then?** Let's say it's evolved relative to conte(n/x)t. **How did you decide on the format? Did you go through different stages? Why this format and not another?** We wanted make something which would be everything to everybody masquerading as a book about why we do what we do. Progress was slow until we realised most people would actually prefer a book about why we do what we do masquerading as something which could be everything to everybody. **How long is the book, let's say, in terms of pages? How did you make this decision?** 324 because it is the new number of the beast … you choose. **Are you going to be using many 'specials'? Which ones?** Yes. All of them, as and when necessary. **Format Vs Content, what's more important? How do the two relate?** Content should dictate format. Sometimes it does. One without the other is like Sheffield without Wednesday (reference to local football team Sheffield Wednesday). **Have you already made up your minds as to the front cover?** Yes. Several times. **What about the title? Is it still Brain Aided Design? And in which case, why this title?** Yes. Brain Aided Design because we do what it says on the cover. It was going to be 'New & Used' or 'Thatcher our part in her downfall'. **What is your relationship with your publisher like?** He buys the beers and we drink them. **Is the book organized in chronological order or in sections or is there any other system?** Chronological. Readers can make their own connections … **When is it the right time for a graphic designer or design group to publish a book?** When they have something worth hearing as opposed to something to say.

When working on the book are you looking backwards at what you've done or forwards at what you want the Designers Republic to be? Where we have been is at most a map to where we want to go. Brain Aided Design is a statement of intent, a coming of age, a graduation. It is unfinished. A portfolio for potential clients, a bible for new designers and a jazz mag for boy typographers. **How much of the book is new work? Have you re-worked some of the old work?** New perspectives on used ideas. **How was it looking at things you were doing a few years back? Did you still think the work relevant?** Exhilarating. To us, every breath we've ever taken will always be relevant. It's why we are where we are, creatively. **What was the criteria for deciding what goes in and what is left out?** Something akin to 'describe yourself in ten words …' **How were the decisions taken? And who took them?** Empirically. The Designers Republic. **Is there a text to go with the book? Who wrote it? Is it a history of the company? An interview? A commentary on your work?** There are several texts being considered. The history is told through the work selected and the accompanying captions complemented by press quotes. The texts are intended to deal with the philosophy, not the facts.

Do you feel your work and in general the work of graphic designers gets proper critical recognition? Have you read anything about your work which you thought was insightful? It's about the work not the recognition. What we do, we do for us, and hopefully the client. We don't seek critical approval, but of course we do love having our egos massaged. Probably the most insightful writing about our work is by people who connect with our ideas and actually write about their own feelings … People who write purely about our design miss the point. **How do you think the book will affect people's perception of your work?** Some people will be surprised by the scope of our activity … **Do you have any special events scheduled along with the launch of the book?** We're planning on going out for a few drinks.

* * *

The Designers Republic book, **Brain Aided Design**, will be published by Laurence King Publishing at some point in the not so distant future.

Inside /
The Designers Republic

Inside /
page 35

Inside /
Interview

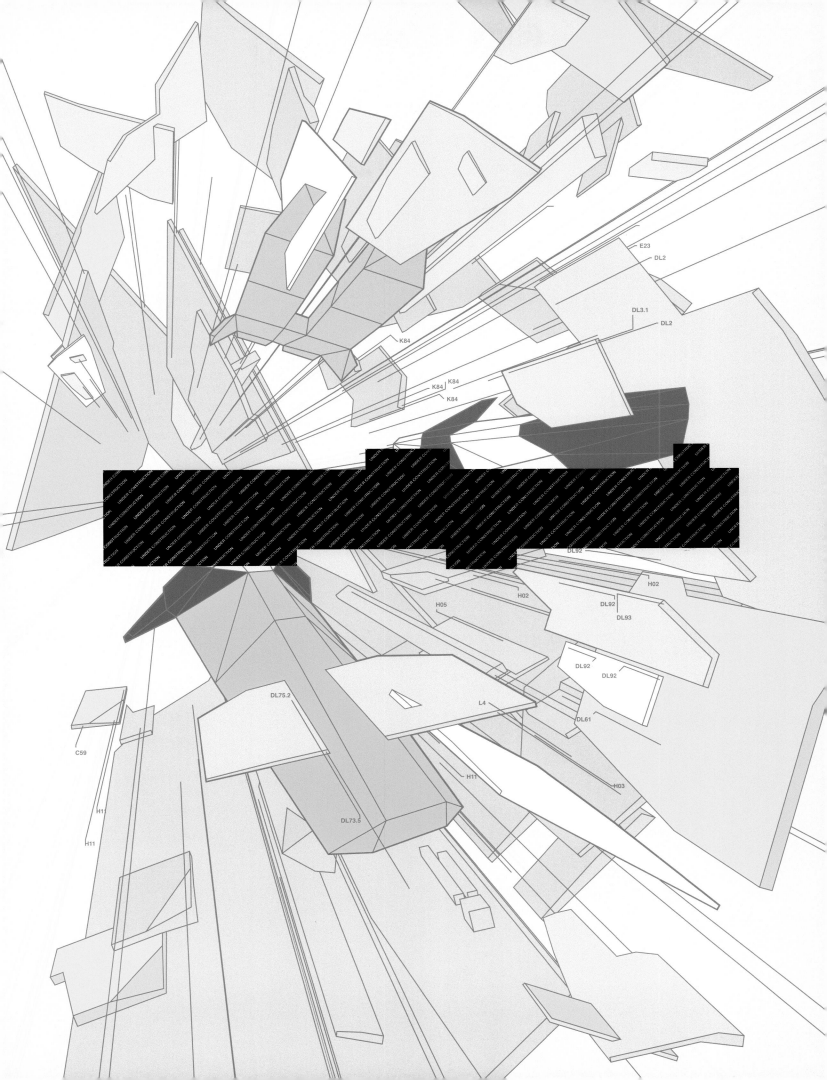

Profile / Eley Kishimoto

interview with Mark Eley
by Lachlan Blackley

Eley Kishimoto have established themselves as a vibrant and positive force in the fashion industry, with their colourful print-based textile and fashion design. The company was formed by Mark Eley and Wakako Kishimoto in 1992 and continues a more traditional practice of textile printing from a small studio workshop in South London. As well as their own collections, Eley Kishimoto have collaborated with many high profile designers, including Alexander McQueen, Marc Jacobs and Hussein Chalayan. A recent retrospective of their work at the V&A museum revealed a prolific output, that also includes interior products: wallpaper, furniture, ceramics and glass, along with luggage and other accessories. Mark talks with us about the process of design, telling stories through print and future collaborative work.

What roles do each of you play within the company? Eley Kishimoto is fundamentally 8 people that have as much equal importance in the operational aspect of the company – there's no focus on either of us. Obviously the name is me and Wak but the roles and responsibilities are equally distributed. We see it as a group. We've always seen it as a group even though the group has got bigger and bigger with increased demands on what's going on, with productivity and activity within the company. And it's all mixed up. There are levels of production, there's levels of administration, there's levels of physical design and development, which are factions within it – but there's no need to understand it. It's just the product of Eley Kishimoto. We will always stay small. I can never imagine more than, say, fifteen people working here at once.

What is your reason for keeping it small? We need to keep our handwriting very, very intimate. We could take on many projects, we could take on many consultancies, but by bringing in more people to actually start designing we start to lose the handwriting. By keeping it small and intimate we have control of our output and also our aesthetic. There's no need really, to go out there and communicate widely, because it would dampen the identity that we put out. And also, perhaps there's not the demand really, at the end of the day. **Is it about keeping to your creativity as opposed to the industry taking over and dictating what you produce?** Everything that we produce can be produced in mass volume. From the very beginning we've always had the idea that as designers we're here to communicate and we have a responsibility to ourselves. We've put ourselves in this world to basically communicate a one-off piece, knowing that that one-off piece can actually be put into mass manufacture and hold the same integrity. So, therefore, we're not frightened of the mass – it's part and process of being a designer. If your thing becomes available to mass, obviously there's logistics with regards to pricing and the productivity behind the product on that level which creates restrictions. But, if it does go to mass, your ideology goes out to a larger audience. And I think what we have to say is actually fundamentally quite simple to understand, so the actual communication doesn't restrict it in its development or the distance it can travel.

01

02

Inside /
Eley Kishimoto

Inside /
page 40

Inside /
Profile

03

OUTSIDE / NICK KNIGHT

'I HOPE THAT WHAT
WE COMMUNICATE
GIVES OTHER PEOPLE
MOTIVATION TO WANT
TO PRODUCE THEIR
OWN WORK OR WANT
TO COMMUNICATE
SOMETHING
CREATIVELY ACTIVE –
IT'S A POSITIVE THING.'

OUTSIDE / NEW YORK

OUTSIDE / FILMS

What is that fundamental thing you want to communicate? I hope that what we communicate gives other people motivation to want to produce their own work or want to communicate something creatively active – it's a positive thing. And it's also to try to create and make people comfortable with their own intelligence with regards to understanding aesthetics. So it's fundamentally a very motivational development idea – not to kind of restrict, but to open up. **You formed in 1992. Did you set out with this ideology from the beginning or is it something that's developed?** Myself and Wak met in 1989, and even though we both did textiles (I was a weaver, Wak's a printer) and we were both focused on fashion, we were looking at the wider arts at that stage. We were just hanging out together at exhibitions, and we were motivated by dance and stuff like that. When we formed we didn't have a real manifesto to get Eley Kishimoto together. We just wanted to form a studio because we felt unemployable and we wanted to get to grips with the fundamental craft of our work where we set up looms and we set up print tables, and got involved in chemicals and stuff. At that particular time, textile designers were just working on paper

Inside /
Eley Kishimoto

Inside /
page 41

Inside /
Profile

04

05

06

and they actually didn't understand the product they were trying to create. So we just set up this precedent that we'd actually work directly to cloth and looked at putting it towards product. So we actually have a relation to the thing that touches the customer directly. Perhaps that was the starting point of getting close to, or taking the responsibility to communicate directly, because they would actually be touching our product. I think that touching the product has always been close to us — that we'd rather get the customer to touch our product, than the magazine or media or promotional activity. It's always about trying to get our product out there.

Your work is about strong colour, bold prints and big form which contrasts to the more mainstream subtle or sombre tendencies of fashion. Is that a reflection of your personalities? Have you always designed that way, and did you set out to do that? No, when we first started what was around us was a lot of technique driven work, a lot of deconstruction, a lot of fabric manipulation. It didn't really deal with pattern that much. If you look within the mainstream, or within facets of the avant-garde, there is always pattern within fashion. It never disappears and sometimes, even when it's in deconstructive work or fabric manipulation work, it exists, but it's a lot more subtle. We started to go against that to a certain degree because we felt we had the ability to actually do something which felt fresh. We wanted to create something which actually looked slightly different. We wanted to do something which wasn't a part of mode — we wanted to be independent. And we weren't frightened of being independent, as we thought, basically, that would set up an identity for us, which would stay true to a certain degree. And we could use it as a platform to get to the stage where we could deal with the strength of identity — with things that are very bold or very informative, to things that are very, very sensitive and very subtle. We have the range within our work now. At the beginning it wasn't so much like that, it was a little bolder throughout. With the prints themselves, we're not frightened of the brashness or the information that goes out there. But I do think, as we mature, it's becoming a lot more sensitive. **Why do you think that is?** I think it's just our maturity, and maybe we're softening our edges ourselves. There's a kind of responsibility to commercialism, a responsibility to survival with regards to going forwards in the industry. And also maybe a move within ourselves about making things, I don't know…more like ourselves. More like what we're thinking now.

> 'WITH THE PRINTS THEMSELVES, WE'RE NOT FRIGHTENED OF THE BRASHNESS OR THE INFORMATION THAT GOES OUT THERE. BUT I DO THINK, AS WE MATURE, IT'S BECOMING A LOT MORE SENSITIVE.'

Do you feel that you have a lot of freedom with what you do or do you sometimes feel limited by the industry? We've always designed our work for fashion under restriction. We have a responsibility to our activity with regards to what we can physically produce after we make a model. Once the model's made that has to sell and then go into production. And the actual responsibility to the production of that model we calculate within the model-making and then those restrictions are always in place — one with colours, one with fabric, one with availability of fabric and actual quality of manufacture in relationship to its price. So, it's an engineered item we're trying to create which has a responsibility to actually put it out into the market. It's a commercial item. Therefore that's our restriction and that's always been in place.

Where do you draw inspiration from? Daily existence. It's trying to find a quality of life. It's trying to get motivation everyday, being as kind a person to everybody as you possibly can. To understand quality of life with your family as well as with your work, travel, everyday living. Getting on the bus, going to work, talking to the newspaper guy — that's inspiration. It's like a matter of getting up every morning and going to work…its good enough.

In terms of the actual prints, do you reference things or are there things that inform your aesthetic? No. Obviously there are things which we digest, that we retrieve at certain points. We're not that cultured company couple or whatever with regards to what's going on in the outside world. We don't go to all the exhibitions. We do read books. We do understand what's gone on in the past within textiles. With regards to inspiration, we go along a route where we create or

Inside /
Eley Kishimoto

Inside /
page 42

Inside /
Profile

she doesn't know whether they're there by choice or whether they're forced to be there. So she joins the queue to find out and then she sees this procession of transformation. Obviously burying into that is the idea of women turning into butterflies and transformation with regards to the relationship to clothes and cosmetics. And today's expectations of society upon women is obviously imbued within all of that. As she gets closer to her own transformation she starts to become aware that it's a non-reality. It's a dream. But then she goes into this spin of not knowing if she's in non-reality or reality, because she's waking up from this idea. We're undecided about our own commitment to transformation through society's pressure or our own kind of understanding of our choices. We go through the second phase of thinking about what's going on and the confusion about non-reality and reality. So within the collection you get this kind of digested information of things which are out of focus, things which are possibly photographic but non-photographic, things which are crafted but are then just off-centre, things which are in front of or past issues – loyalties to other things we've done in our past work. And then basically she wakes up. She has her pyjamas on, she gets her white shirt on and she goes to work.

Can you tell me more about the Show Studio project, Screen Prints? What was your response to that? That was really cool, I loved the Show Studio project. It was thirteen films by thirteen very, very current contemporary stylists, art directors, filmmakers, and photographers. We assessed all the contributors work together with Show Studio. And, from the levels of principles of their work, we made decisions and said, 'OK, they should have that

print and they should have that print…' We decided what product to send to them relative to what they do and then they had complete creative freedom to produce their work. With the idea of working with 13 different personalities, I thought I didn't want to get more involved than actually just passing the product and being really open with how they interpreted it. And I was really intrigued by how people would interpret our work in their own way. There's levels within our work I see, that don't get put out there with the way we actually communicate ourselves – with the likes of sex, darkness, the macabre, lightness. All those aspects maybe we communicate in a product, but we actually don't tell people or it's not digested that way. Whereas in the Show Studio project I thought people interpreted it in a huge spectrum, and there's levels and principles of that interpretation I actually felt really comfortable with. The people with the fish (Michelle Duguid and Adam Mufti), I thought that was hilarious, the way they interpreted the brief. The Felix Larher piece with the sex in chains – I thought that was strong. And Norbert Schoerner's Flash, with regards to using it as a virus. There were very, very clever interpretations there. www.showstudio.com

Finally what questions shouldn't I ask you in an interview? 'What kind of woman do you dress?' At the end of the day the classic saying is, 'We just dress girls who know a thing or two'. And never ask me what my favourite colour is. **Do people ask you that?** Yeah! you'd be surprised; 'What's your favourite colour?' **What else?** Oh my God, I could go through so many…'What's in your secret address book?' And I'd say 'Secrets' now. **What's the idea of asking that one…?** Yeah, we've got so many interviews that we just say no to, or we're antagonistic back.

* * *

09
Damask Typical Eley
Kishimoto Hobnob side chair

10
Flash Typical Eley Kishimoto
Hobnob

11–14
EK Look book
Produced by HarrimanSteel
(in newspaper format) is sent

to the buyers so they can
preview the collections and
prints. In collaboration with
EK they also design the show
invites, posters, seat packs
and packaging.
www.harrimansteel.co.uk

15–17
Spring/Summer Collection
2004

15

16

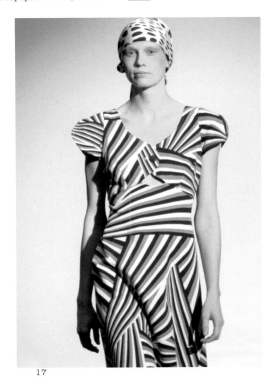

17

**Inside/
Eley Kishimoto**

**Inside/
page 47**

**Inside/
Profile**

Textfield

Edition 3, Spring 2004 | 15 USD, 12 Euro

http://www.textfield.org

Look /
Read /
Use

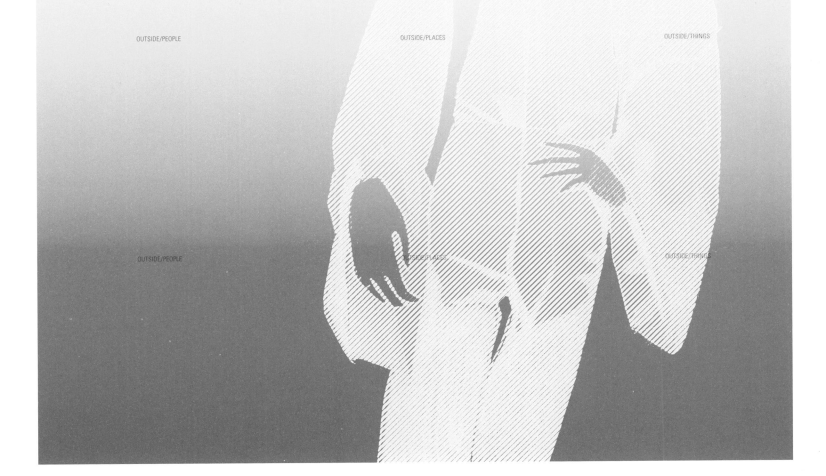

Zara Wood
Less Rain
Dan Tobin Smith
Borja Martinez
Insect
Inca Starzinsky
Daniel Askill
David Foldvari
Chris Gambrell
Marie Lund & Nina Beier
Tatiana Arocha
Emma Hammaren & Michael Evidon
David Earl Dixon
Christian Hundertmark
Clarissa Tossin
Santiago Vanegas

WOOD'S
WORLD

THE WORLD IS FULL OF
RANDOM MEN WITH AN
URGE TO TRANSFORM
YOU INTO A GRINNING
MANIAC. PLEASE RESIST

THE WORLD IS FULL
OF SMALL DOGS
WITH BIG BOWELS

the world is
full of words
like:
nut
allergy
lacto
intollerant
girl
choking
on
yogurt
coated
peanut

Wood's World is a series of personal observations of the world around us. All the work is hand drawn on cardboard. It is rather cynical.

Zara's relationship with her immediate surroundings:
NOT a. harmonious & life-enhancing
NOT b. stimulating & thought provoking
NOT c. largely decorative
NOT d. mutually destructive
NOT e. poor
NOT f. not sure
BUT g. other: mostly good. Often eager to clean it.

Over the last couple of years Woody has been spotted doodling in Melbourne and London. As well as producing illustration commissions for London based fashion labels including Griffin, Parka Rock and Annett Olivieri, Woody continues to do limited edition t-shirt designs for Stussy Australia.

Woody's range of sew-on patches and limited edition handmade toys including the 'Drunk Dolls' series were launched through Fat, voted one of the best retail outlets in Australia by British Vogue 2002. Commissioned by Melbourne based Third Drawer Down, Woody designed an art tea towel entitled 'Fed up of being domestic', made up of various characters you could cut out and take to parties.
Exhibitions include 'Gone to the Dogs' for Saatchi & Saatchi London, where 4ft high Chihuahuas proved they did not know the meaning of being house-trained, 'I just don't skate' for record company City Rockers, 'Good pants, Shame about the Face' for Notting Hill boutique Euforia, 'Cecille's Invincible Wig' for Craft Victoria, Melbourne and 'One for the Money' for the Match Bar chain. You can also find 'Can you see the Wood for the Trees?' on permanent display in Magma Bookshop, Earlham Street, Covent Garden.

woodifshecould@hotmail.com

01

00

02

03

04

05

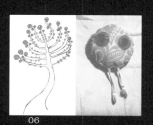

06

07

08

00
Zara Wood
One of the Drunk Dolls;
perhaps an alter-ego

01
Make the Dance Yours
– Swan Lake
First in a series of ads for
Capulet dance wear. 2003

02
Cecille's Invisible Wig
Study for exhibition for
Craft Victoria, Melbourne.
2003

03
One for the Money
Poster / flyer for exhibition.
2003

04
Coco de Mer
Book plate. 2003

05
Stussy Star Suit
Limited edition T-shirt. 2003

06
Tree and Green Toy
Illustration & handmade toy.
2002

07
Tina Turner
A bizarre thought. 2002

08
True Love Always Lion
Fabric print design for True
Love Always. 2004

Less Rain is a creative agency based in London and Berlin. Founded in 1997, Less Rain first came to prominence with www.lessrain.com, a collection of small interactive interfaces linked to the spine of Walter the Fish. Since then, Less Rain has worked with Sony Playstation, Channel 4, Red Bull, Mitsubishi, Haribo, Scottish Courage and the V&A Museum. Latest projects include www.fashionfringe.co.uk, www.i-shake-u.com and www.vandalsquad.com.

reception@lessrain.com
www.lessrain.co.uk

Less Rain's relationship with their immediate surroundings:
NOT a. harmonious & life-enhancing
NOT b. stimulating & thought provoking
NOT c. largely decorative
NOT d. mutually destructive
NOT e. poor
NOT f. not sure
BUT g. other: preventing a clean shot, needs to be taken down.

The LRPD Vandal Squad: working for a clean environment.
15.12.2003

Over the past several years, graffiti vandalism has exploded across the Internet, costing the industry millions of dollars.
To answer this threat, Less Rain has founded in 2002 its own police department, the LRPD, with a special anti-graffiti task force, the Vandal Squad.
Formerly known mostly for its graphic design, Less Rain has now a structure in place that allows for a creative eradication of not only graffiti but also the vandals behind it and, of course, those who harbor them.
To reinforce our argument, we have recently added M113 APCs and AH-1T+ Super Cobras to our fleet. Our submission for Graphic 04 is an impressive display of our determination for a clean, safe, graffiti-free environment, as well as a public call for support. Help the LRPD. Become a supporter now; otherwise it might be too late. For information on our public awareness program, please visit www.vandalsquad.com

00

03

01

02

04

stitch here

05

06

07

08

00
LRPD – Protecting your neighbourhood since 2002.

01
Beck's Futures website
www.becksfutures.co.uk

02
Untitled (Harz, Germany)
Photograph by Andrew Cross, shortlisted for Beck's Futures '04.

03, 04
I-Shake-U
website for Mitsubishi Motors, Japan.
www.i-shake-u.com

05, 06
Fashion Fringe website.
www.fashionfringe.co.uk

07, 08
Vandal Squad website.
www.vandalsquad.com
Spray on the original NY subway trains, the Berlin Wall, and more…

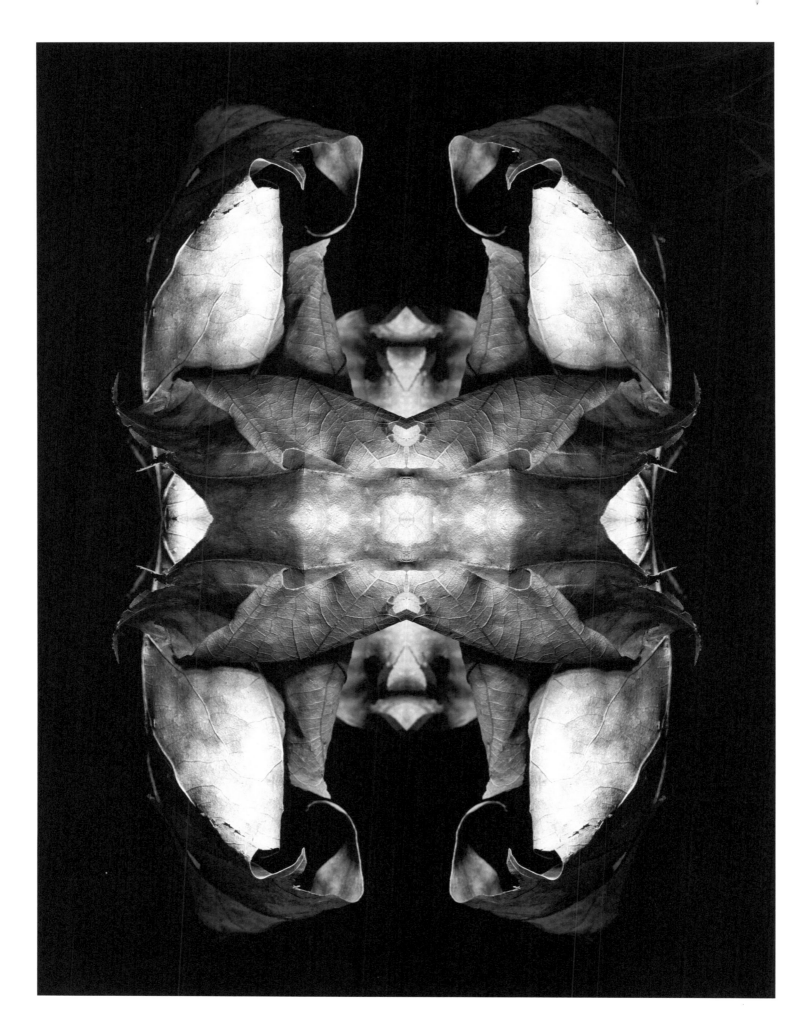

<u>Leaves</u>
2002–2003

Pictures of dead leaves, for an exhibition at Lapidarium Gallery, Prague, 2002. Collected dead leaves and photographed them with the purpose of using parts of the pictures as montages to create patterns within the final images. Influenced by the system of the golden section.

Dan's relationship with his immediate surroundings:
NOT c. largely decorative
NOT e. poor
NOT f. not sure
NOT g. other:
BUT a. harmonious & life-enhancing
AND b. stimulating & thought provoking
AND d. mutually destructive

Dan Tobin Smith was brought up in London, and started taking pictures at the age of 13. He took a foundation course at Central Saint Martins and then a degree in photography at the London College of Printing. Graduating in 1999, Dan began to shoot commercially and later started developing his own still life projects. Influenced by legendary photographers Bill Brandt, Lennart Nilsson and Josef Sudek, Dan is constantly working on his own personal projects which range from studio work to landscape and interiors. Dan joined the Katy Barker Agency at the end of 2003 and has so far worked with Arena Homme +, French Vogue, 10, and Wallpaper, and has worked with advertising clients such as Volkswagon, Swiss, Tate, Orange and Swarovski.

00

01

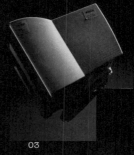
03

04

02

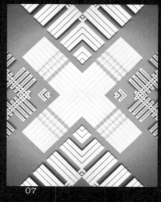
07

05

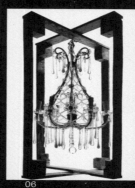
06

00
Dan Tobin Smith

01
From: <u>Under Cover</u>
interiors still life story for
Wallpaper March Issue 04.
Interiors Editor: Leila Latchin

02
For Paris Vogue, Catherine
Deneuve tribute issue.
Creative Director: Fabien
Barron

03
Untitled, 2003.
Personal Work

04,05
Untitled series, Sweden 2003.
Personal Work.

06
For Liberty's, 2003.
Stylist: Emma Dahlman.

07
For Wallpaper, still life story.
Interiors editor: Roberta Holm

I was born in Barcelona where I studied Product Design until 1996. During those years I combined my design studies with musical interests, and played bass for several years.

Later on I began to focus my interests in Graphic Design and decided to move to London where I began a BA degree in Graphic & Media Design (Experimental Typography) at The London College of Printing. During this past 3 years I have been combining my design studies with work experience in a London-based design firm. I'm currently working as a freelance designer, doing a vast variety of projects: from CD covers to corporate identities for bars and restaurants, or charity foundations. I believe designers should constantly investigate new forms of communication; therefore nowadays I divide my time between commercial work and personal projects.

Borja's relationship with his immediate surroundings:
NOT c. largely decorative
NOT d. mutually destructive
NOT e. poor
NOT f. not sure
NOT g. other:
NOT a. harmonious & life-enhancing
BUT b. stimulating & thought provoking

Sand Stencils, Mallorca
&
Spray Adhesive
Stencill, London
01.2002–03.2003

My work is a mixture of Product Design and Graphic Design. The original idea normally comes from a graphic concept, only to be converted into a volumetric object, and then back into a flat surface. Never forgetting one of my main goals, which is to communicate using the elements that surround us in everyday life. I'm very much attached to the idea of craftsmanship in graphic design. That is the reason why stencils play an important role in my work.

I use some of my personal projects to comment on political or social issues, using the power of graphics with propagandistic purposes.

I believe it is important to keep a childlike enthusiasm towards our surroundings, In order to produce fresh work that will surprise other people.

01

00

02

03

04

05

06

07

08

CONSUMERISM
MAY
DAMAGE
YOUR
HEALTH

THIS
ISLAND
IS
50%
SAND

TRUTH
IS ARRIVED AT
THROUGH
THE OBSERVATION
OF NATURE

WE ARE WHAT WE EAT

pages 76–78
The Hills Have Eyes
(Wall A & Wall B)

Last summer we worked with
men's clothing label Gravy
co-designing a range of
printed Ts and sweats.
We were approached by
Dreambagsjaguarshoes,
a bar in Shoreditch, to put on
an exhibition inspired by the
graphic themes we had used
as prints. These included
backwoods hicksville horror,
the texas chainsaw massacre
and movies like Deliverance
and Southern Comfort.

    pages 79–81
The Hills Have Eyes:
Claw Forest

These two pieces were
produced for the website
www.picturesonwalls.com
set up buy Banksy and Steve
Lazarides from SleazeNation.
They were printed as seven-
colour silkscreen prints,
and the brief was completely
open.
We were told to come up with
something suitably 'Dark &
Twisted'!

Insect's relationship with their immediate surroundings:
NOT a. harmonious & life-enhancing
NOT b. stimulating & thought provoking
NOT c. largely decorative
NOT d. mutually destructive
NOT e. poor
NOT f. not sure
BUT g. other: organised chaos

Luke Davies and Paul
Humphrey set up London-
based design collective
Insect 6 years ago, after
discovering their mutual
admiration for all things
six-legged, dark and twisted.
From their ivy-covered nest
in EC1, they mix illustration,
photography, typography
and taxidermy in their
work for the youth market

and music industry. Over
the past year they have
also been concentrating
on commercially available
screen prints for
picturesonwalls.com and
for exhibitions in London,
Paris, New York and Tokyo.
2004 will also see a small
collection of Insect clothing
and merchandise, and the
first live London outing as
The House Of Fix, their
deranged electronic alter-
ego signed to Berlin's Tresor
Records. Their clients range
from small independent
record companies to global
brands like BBC, Orange,
Motorola and Levi's.

info@insect.co.uk
www.insect.co.uk

00

01

03

02

06

08

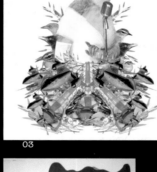

05

00
Luke Davies &
Paul Humphrey

01
Orange Mobile 60
Christmas Campaign
Agency: Mother

02
Dr Who Re-branding
illustrations
BBC Worldwide

03
Mish Mash
flyer
01.2004

04
Insect target poster
screen print detail
www.picturesonwalls.com

05
Source of Wonder
screen print
www.day14.com

06
Insect target poster
screen print detail
www.picturesonwalls.com

07
House of Fix Album
Tresor Records

08
Archive Album (Noise)
ie: music

ided   Inca's relationship with her immediate surroundings:
NOT e. poor
NOT f. not sure
NOT g. other:
NOT a. harmonious & life-enhancing
NOT b. stimulating & thought provoking
NOT c. largely decorative
BUT d. mutually destructive (but that's the landlord's fault)

Look Around
An ongoing project

A series of patterns which
act as visual demonstrations
of various statistics. The
patterns are then applied to
appropriate objects, thereby
making their messages
accessible and visible to all.

00

01

02

03

after 6

04

05

06

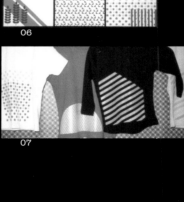

07

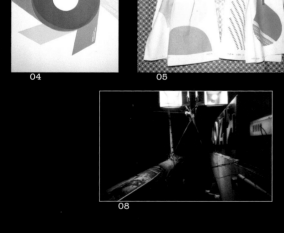

08

06
Mufti self-promotional cards
Screenprints

04
After 6 poster
Exhibition of printmakers
in residence at Central St
Martins College, London.
Screenprint, 2003

07
Mufti T-shirts
Mufti was co-founded in 2002
with Samuel Baker.
2002, 2003
www.muftiday.co.uk

00
Inca Starzinsky

01, 02
Wooden landscapes
Photographs, 2002

03
Homage to DS
Series of three screenprints
based on my photographs of
glass sculptures by Dietrich
Starzinsky, 2002

05
Mufti bags
Screenprints, 2003

08
Ishikawa-dai,
Tokyo

Each person in the UK consumes, on average,
136 plastic carrier bags ( ) per year.

Each person in Germany consumes, on average,
42 plastic carrier bags ( ) per year.

Most of these bags are used only once. The useful
life of a cotton carrier bag is about 10 to 15 years.

THE SECOND RITUAL
BETWEEN

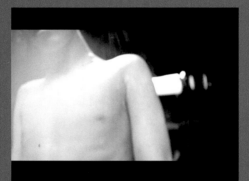

<u>We Have Decided Not To Die</u> is about a mental state where logic drops away and anything is possible. It is an audio visual narrative that uses sound, stunts and visual effects to create a world where characters float in space and time. It tells the story of three characters' modern day journeys of transcendence; journeys into a place where death is no longer inevitable.

Daniel's relationship with his immediate surroundings:

NOT a. harmonious & life-enhancing
NOT b. stimulating & thought provoking
NOT c. largely decorative
NOT d. mutually destructive
NOT e. poor
NOT f. not sure
BUT g. other: shifting

Born in Sydney in 1977, Daniel Askill has worked internationally as a director of commercials, short films and music videos. In addition to this his background in music led him to releases his first album as composer / producer at 19, while also designing record sleeves and multimedia projects.

Initially studying design in Sydney and later at Central Saint Martins in London, Daniel was picked up as creative director of London agency Williams before completing his studies. During his time there he helmed a wde variety of projects from web design for infamous fashion star Alexander McQueen to directing his first commercial for the 'desire' fragrance by Alfred Dunhill.

In 2001 Daniel returned to Sydney to co-found film and design collective COLLIDER. This has led to directing work for clients such as MTV, Virgin, Warner Music & 2day FM. Through COLLIDER he has also continued to develop a number of other award winning personal film projects; the most recent receivning full funding from the Australian Film Commission.

We Have Decided Not To Die recently won the audience prize at the prestigious Clermont-Ferrand short film festival in France.

01

00

02

03

04

...udapest, Hungary
...ber 1973.
...the UK in May
...rently living in
...and working as
...ator as part of the
...family. Education
...Communications
...he people I've
...r: Nike, Puma,
...House, Penguin,
...ecords, Island
...Dazed&Confused,
..., Telegraph,
...ent, various others.

...idfoldvari.co.uk
...idfoldvari.co.uk

...active.com
...active.com

David's relationship with his immediate surroundings:
NOT a. harmonious & life-enhancing
NOT b. stimulating & thought provoking
NOT c. largely decorative
NOT d. mutually destructive
NOT e. poor
NOT f. not sure
BUT g. other: suspicious

pages 98, 10...
Jump
12.01.04
Moments before
certain death

pages 99, 10...
Untitled
Experiences / me...
Hungary / Roma...
The project expl...
surroundings yo...
shape who you a...

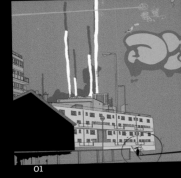

01

02

03

05

06

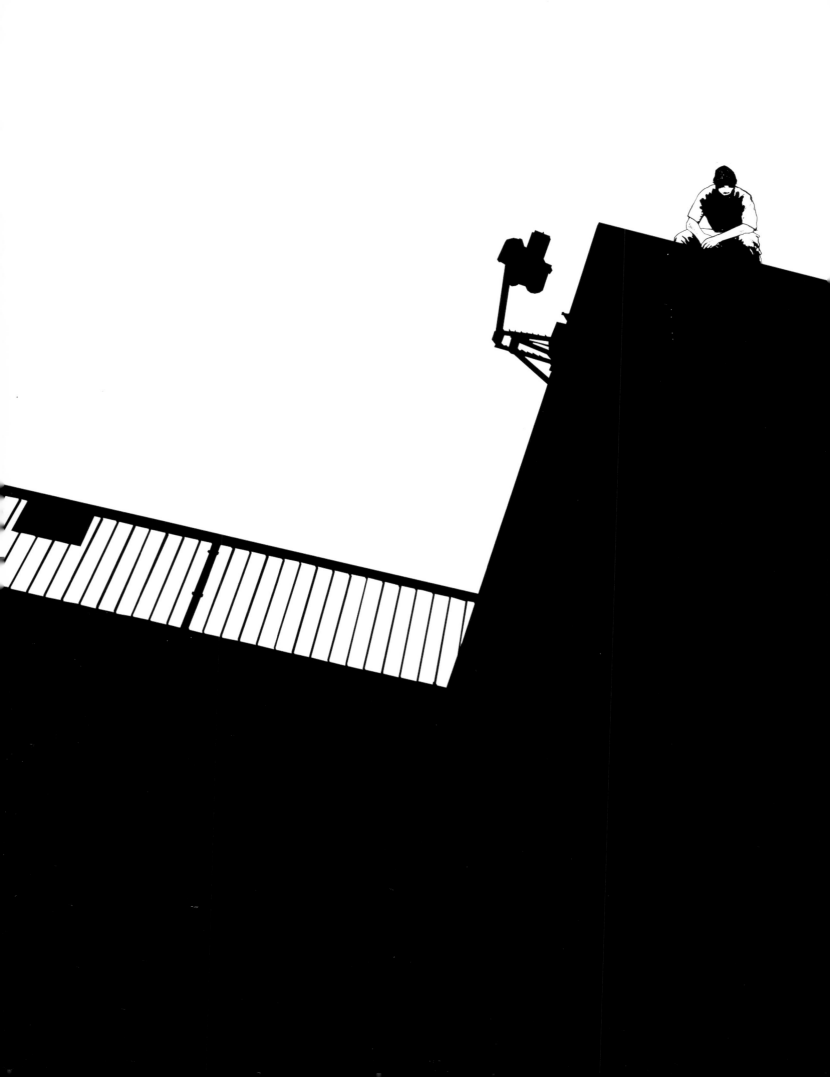

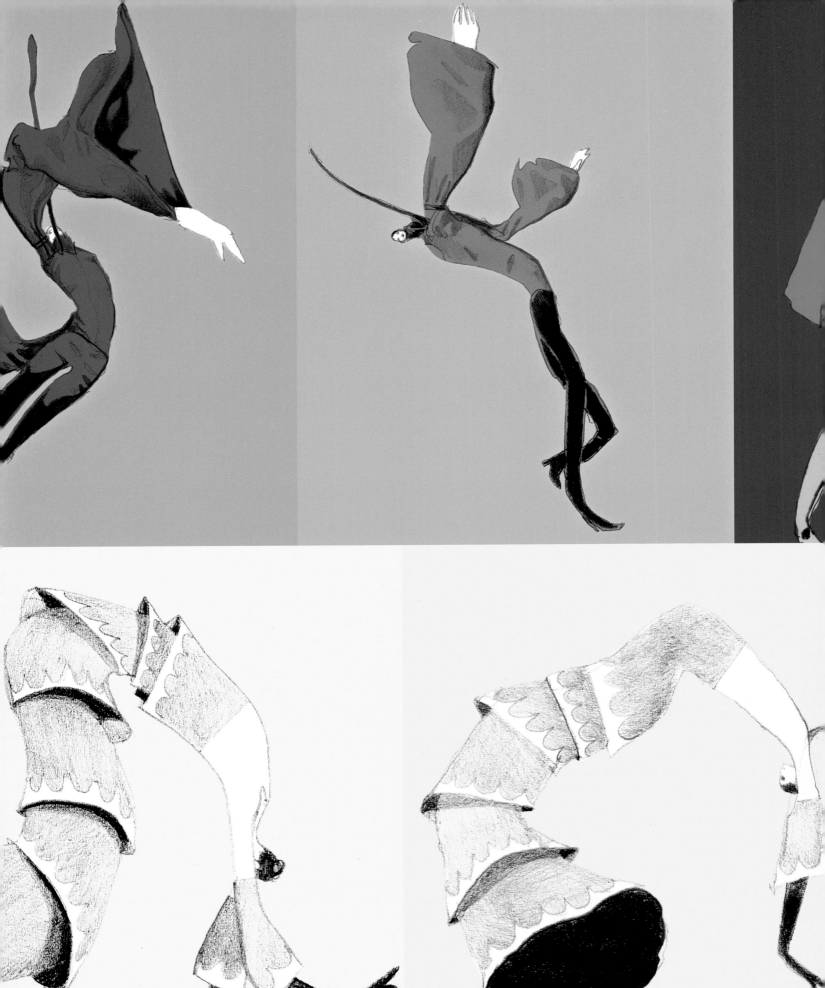

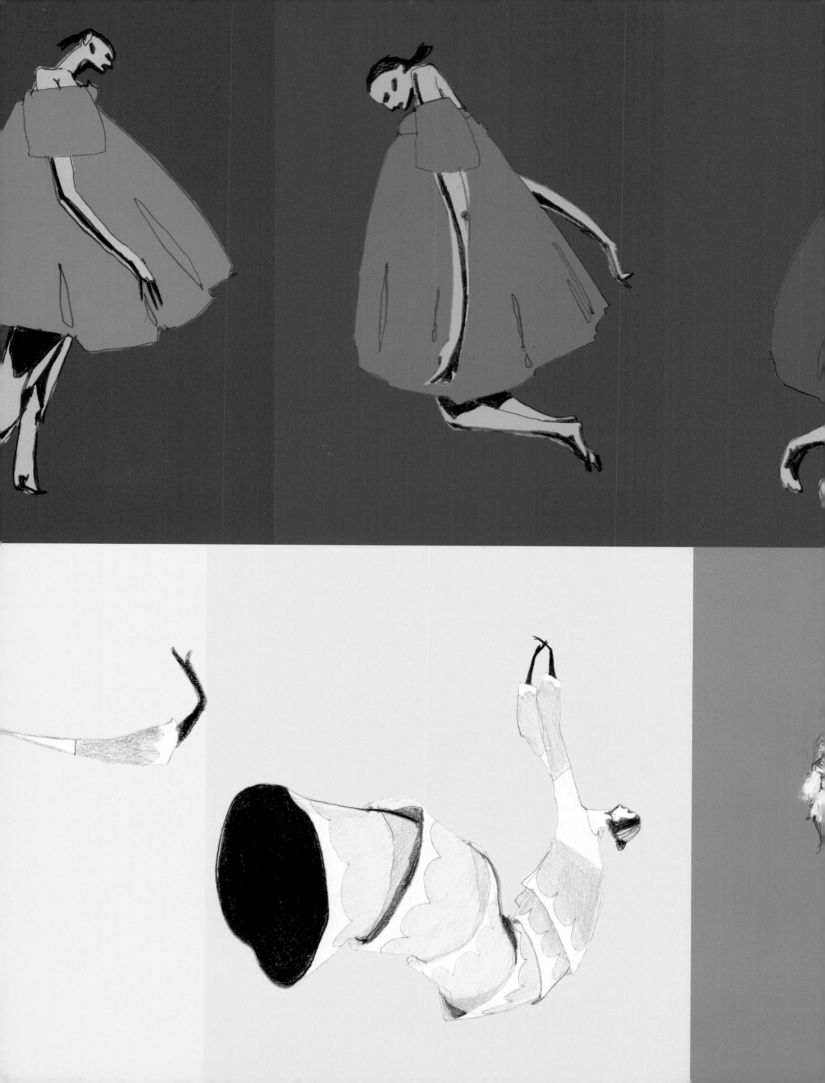

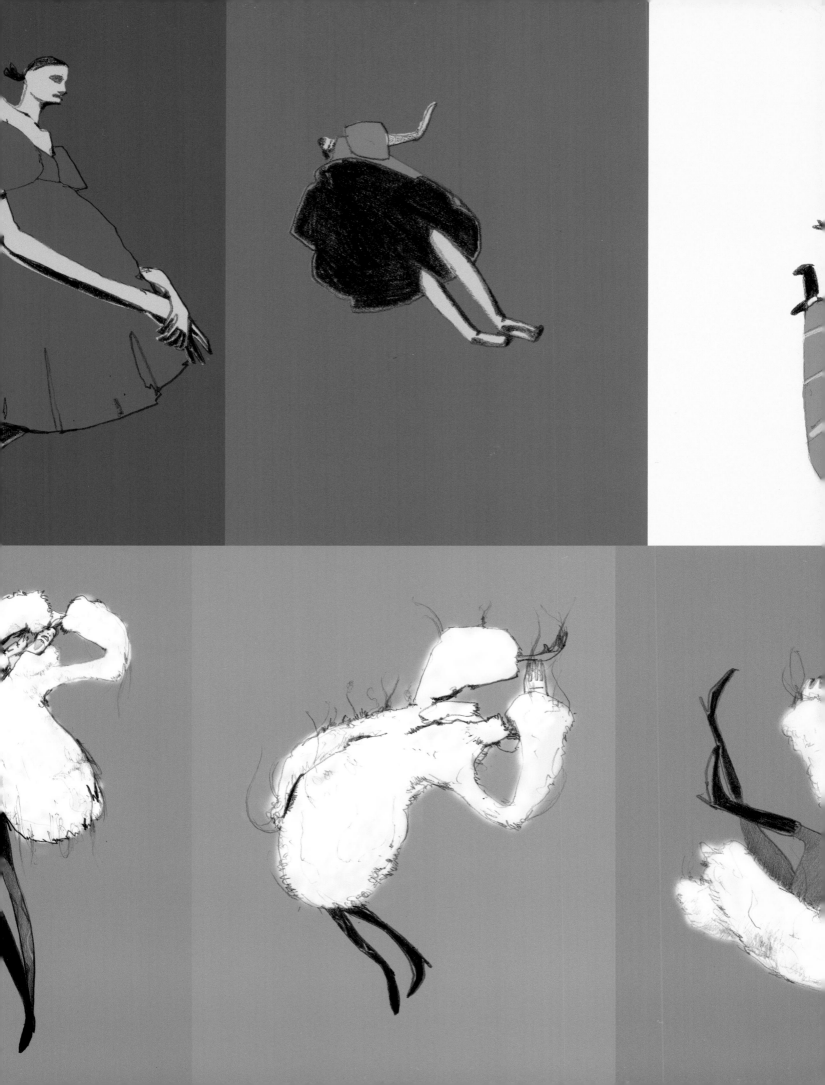

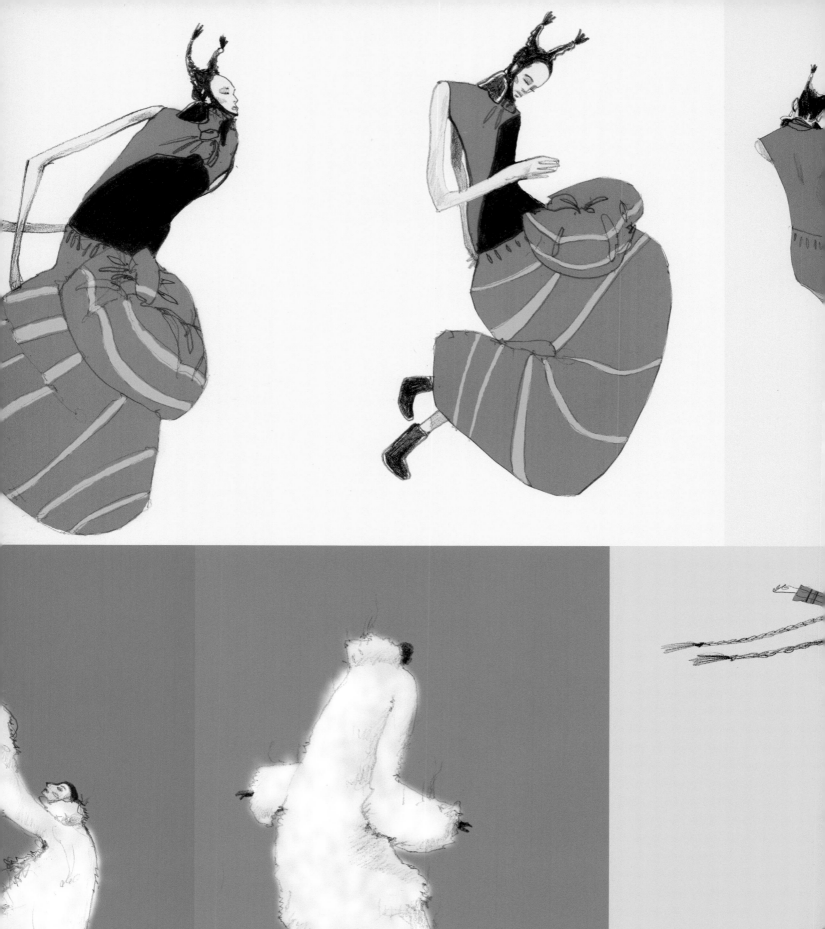

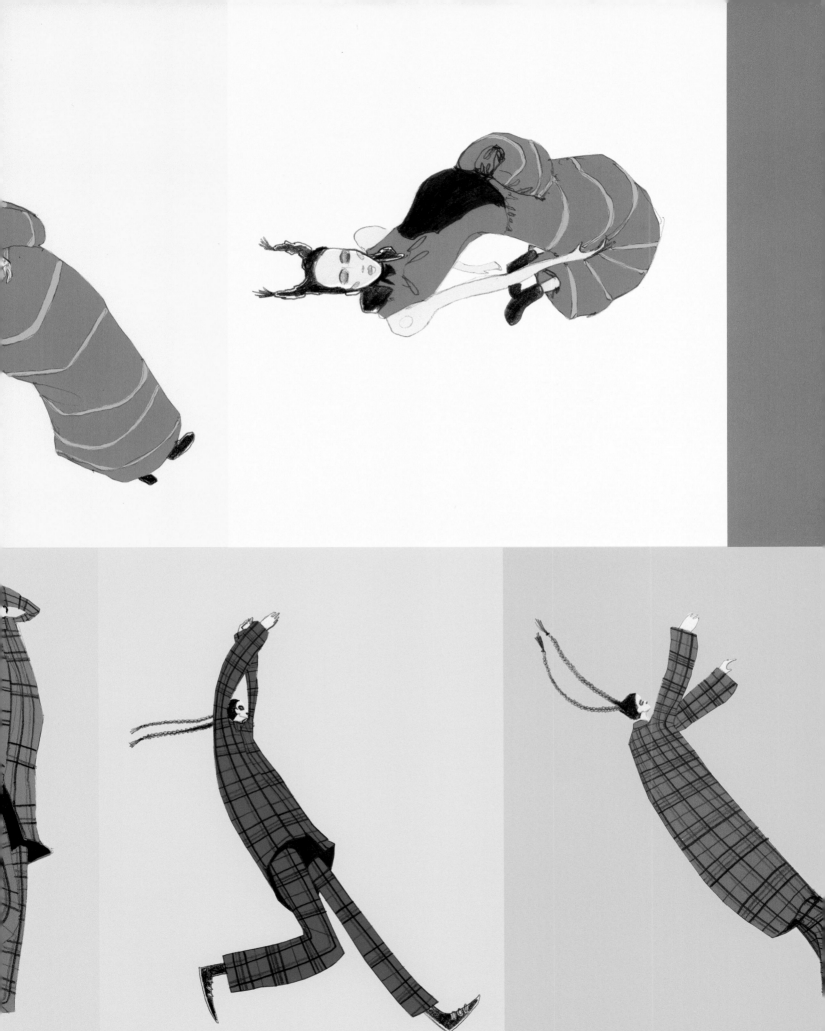

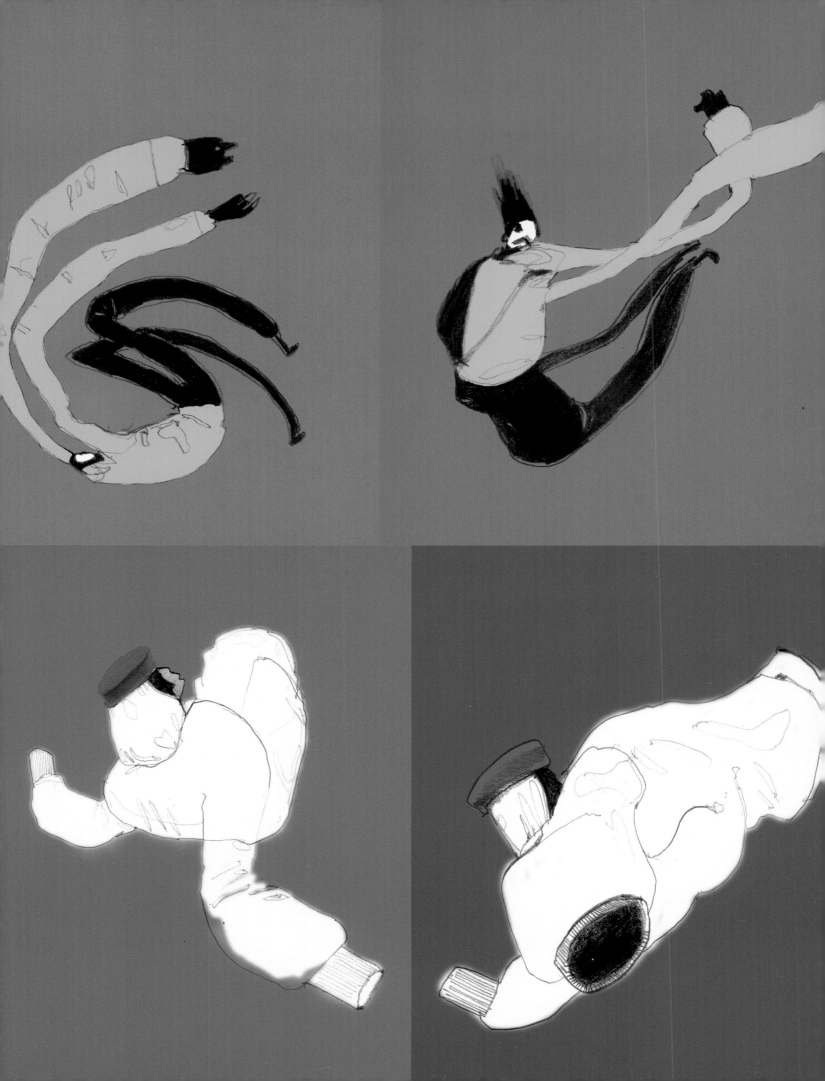

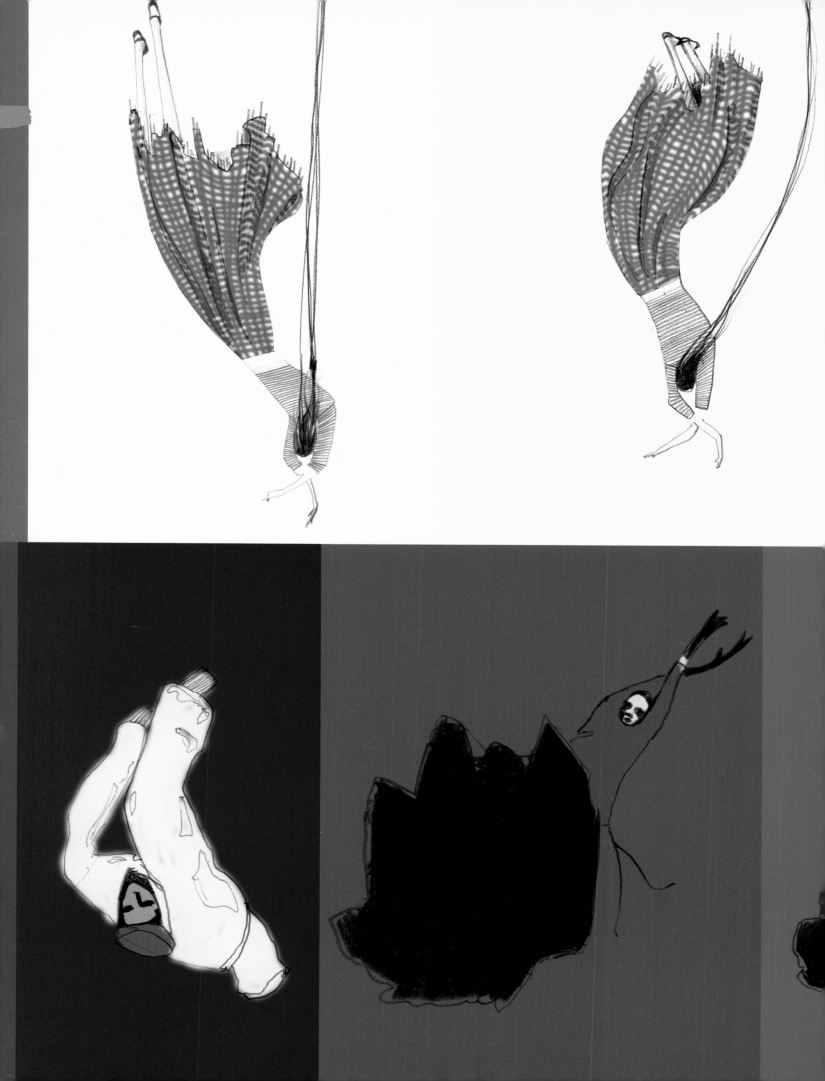

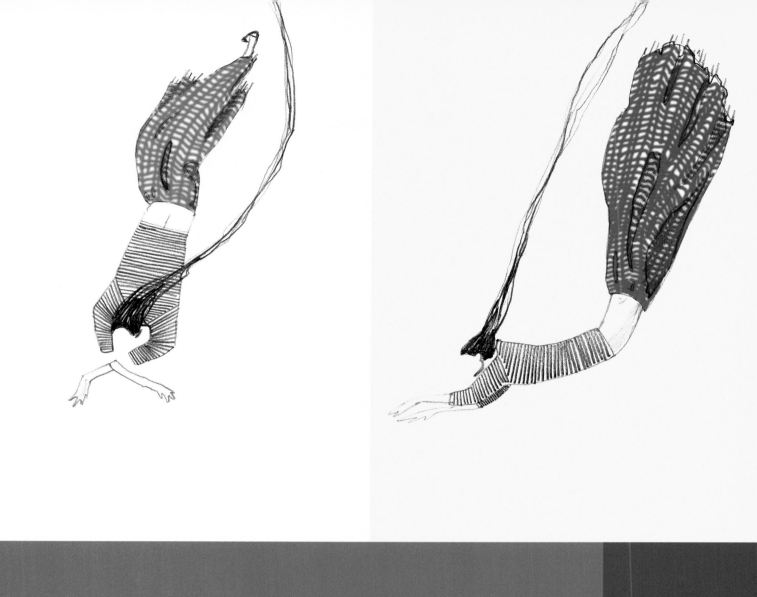
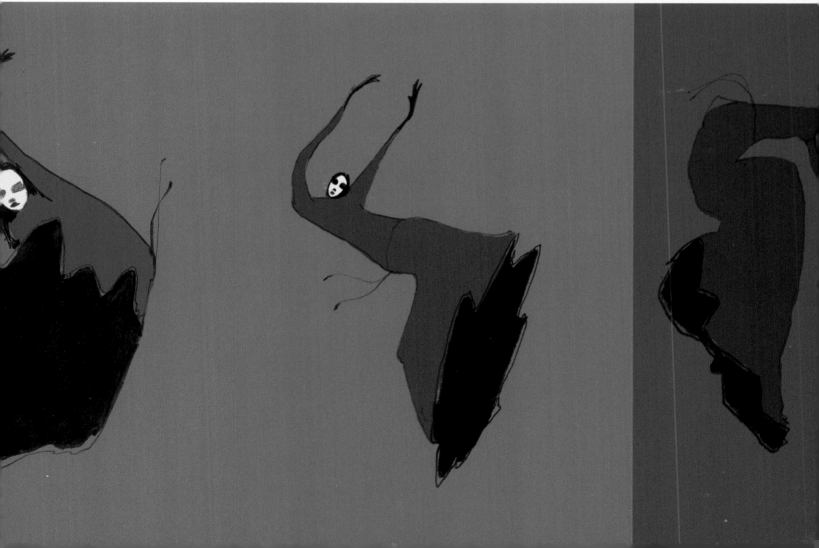

'Falling for' Hintmag
10.2003

Illustration:
Chris Gambrell
Art Direction:
Lee Carter (editor of Hintmag)

This web-based project was an animated selection of 'looks' taken from the Autumn/ Winter collection of 2003. Conceptually based around the notion of falling leaves and the shedding of the old for the new, these Fellini-inspired figures would be portrayed in an erratic flickering downward motion set to music.

A broad selection of looks were chosen yet all of them treated in the same way and subjected to the same freakish distortions. The finished result is something quite different from typical fashion illustration features, layering line work and colours in a very stylised way to create something quite unique.

Chris's relationship with his immediate surroundings:
NOT d. mutually destructive
NOT e. poor
NOT f. not sure
NOT g. other:
NOT a. harmonious & life-enhancing
NOT b. stimulating & thought provoking
BUT c. largely decorative

Chris Gambrell is an illustrator working primarily in the field of fashion since his graduation with an illustration degree in 2001. In addition to his successes in drawing within the fashion industry, Chris has worked on many and varied projects based around corporate imagery / design.

Sketching and recording in books forms a major part of Chris's art process and is evermore dominant in defining the outcome of his thoughts, rather than in the digital tinkering performed towards its end; it is observing form and movement that has led Chris into the area of fashion illustration. Deriving characteristics of line, shape and colour from influences such as Aude Van Ryn, Marion Due Chars and Francois Berthoud, Chris has procured a charismatic style of flamboyant minimalism.

Hintmag, Dresslab and Victionary are just some of the projects Chris has been engaged with over recent months. Chris is also expected to appear in a book featuring 24 of the most innovative fashion illustrators entitled 'Fashionize', to be published later this year. Exhibitions in Bristol, London and Paris have led to Chris' continuing success as a dynamic, fresh and talented young artist.

gambrellchris@aol.com

01

00

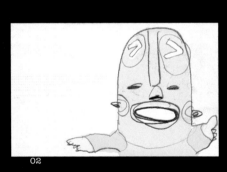

02

03

04

05

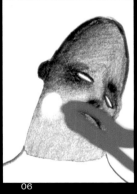

06

07

00
Chris Gambrell

01
Noodle Strudle Nylon
Personal Work

02
Tiki
Personal Work

03
Rafael Lopez
Dresslab

04
Stripe Rendering.
Personal Work

05
Monster
Personal Work

06
Lipstich
Personal Work

07
Fluff
Personal Work

Inside /
pages 138-142

Outside /
David Earl Dixon aka 'Dist'. Essex. Illustrations

pages 138, 139
We see beauty too? /
Old boys brave the snow /
Our homes, our hearts

pages 140, 141
Cold nights, late October /
Whale counting

My work tries to foreground feelings and emotional themes, which we take for granted – the everyday stuff that we forget we do. I try and create characters and creatures that border between contentment and loss – those people who just blend in. I find empathy in the all characters I draw, paint, whatever. I enjoy hiding my cut outs away, obscuring them, framing them within walls and stuff and hopefully someone sees something which they can identify with in some way. Maybe they'll share some kind of loss or a common sense of meandering. The luggage tags came from stickers not sticking. I can just tie them to whatever, railings, lampposts, trees and maybe they just blend in a bit more, become part of my surroundings without anyone really knowing they're there.

David's relationship with his immediate surroundings:
NOT c. largely decorative
NOT d. mutually destructive
NOT e. poor
NOT f. not sure
NOT g. other: organised chaos
NOT a. harmonious & life-enhancing
BUT b. stimulating & thought provoking

I grew up in a little village called Gt. Cornard. I studied film in Southampton and adored Ozu, Kurosawa, Miyazaki & contemporaries such as Tarantino and Scorsese. As my degree continued my love of film began to ebb and I rekindled my love for sketching, drawing, and painting. Getting back into it full

steam seemed the only option. Since then, I have shown my work in various things – the Finders Keepers shows especially. Those guys have really got the right idea, really inspiring to hang out with.
I am trying to sort out a solo gig but I'd like the right venue. I have done a couple of self-published books with work in and am working on a new one at the moment with friends: Matt Sewell, D*face, and some other heads. I am doing a show in New York for the Wooster Collective called 'Hollywood Remix' showing in June.

dist_is_quiet@hotmail.com

00

01

02

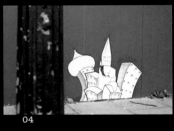

04

03

06

05

08

07

00
David Earl Dixon aka 'Dist'

01
Clown town
Recent dabblings in using a computer.

02
Trees morphed together on the disused curry house piece.

03
Follow bird '84
Late 2003 pillar piece

04
A man of the church hides within an enclosed city.

05
Pirates
Everyone loves pirates, there's one in all of us.

06
More computers, more meandering fancy dress.

07
This guy's just a friendly redneck, he don't mean you no harm.

08
I did this early 2003. The lift looked dull, in a state of dilapidation. I gave it a face.

My name is Christian
Hundertmark (C100)
– 29 years old from Munich,
Germany.
After studying graphic
design and working for
an advertising company I
freelanced for various clients
and design studios. In 2003
I co-founded a design studio,
Backyard10, with work in the
sports and music industry as
well as corporate clients.
I am author and designer of
a book about street art called
'The Art of Rebellion'.
The aim was to open peoples'
eyes to this new art form
happening in cities worldwide.
Beside their brilliant work, it
also gives a nice insight into
the artists themselves with
interviews and shows how
they work.
At the moment I have some
new projects I'm working on.
One is an exhibition and party
concept, called 'The Food
Show'. The idea of this project
is to let Street artists from
all over the world to combine
their work with three topics
'breakfast, lunch and dinner'.
We'll have exhibitions in
Munich and London this year.

www.the-art-of-rebellion.com
www.backyard10.com

Christian's relationship with his immediate surroundings:
NOT b. stimulating & thought provoking
NOT c. largely decorative
NOT d. mutually destructive
NOT e. poor
NOT f. not sure
NOT g. other: organised chaos
BUT a. harmonious & life-enhancing

Rent
01.2004

I'm looking for a new flat
to rent. I recently had a
very interesting offer for
a flat but I didn't get it in
the end because the owner
didn't want to have dogs in
his house. unfortunately
he didn't see my little dog
(I also included him in the
layout), maybe he'd have
changed his opinion then…
Weird?

00

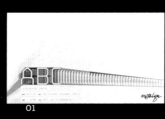

01

02

03

05

04

07

08

06

00
Christian Hundertmark

01
ABC
Club flyer for a monthly
club night

02
The Art of Rebellion
Book

03
Intrudas – Penetrate the
empty space
Artwork for a CD

04
Raptile – Da basilisk's eye
Artwork for a LP

05
Canvas
Spraypaint, Letraset for
typography

06
Board designs for North
Kiteboarding

07
'The Food Show' event
Flyer

08
Fantastik Plastik
Club flyer for a monthly
club night

caperino&
peperone
owned by kuntzel + deygas
www.colette.fr

Discuss /
Write /
Comment

Michael Evamy /
Ungraphic Environment

Rosanna Vitiello /
Been There, Done That

James Davis /
Passed Places

'HOW MANY OF
YOUR DESIGN HEROES
HAVE CONTRIBUTED
ANYTHING TO
THE DEBATE?'
Michael Evamy, page 162

Ungraphic Environment

an essay by Michael Evamy

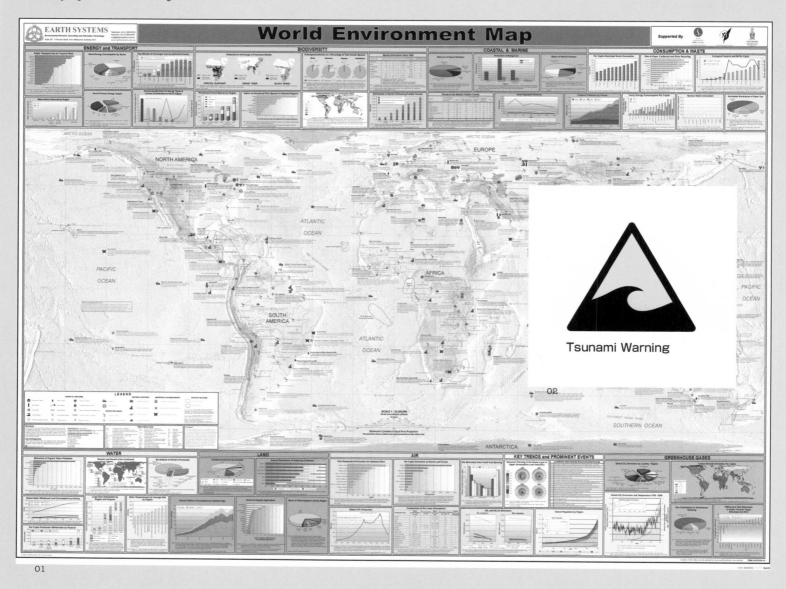

World Environment Map

Tsunami Warning

02

01
World Environment Map,
produced by
Earth Systems

02
Japan National Commitee
for IDNDR Pictogram Project
(PICTO-KEN). Pictogram
system for Natural Disaster
Reduction produced in
collaboration with the
Research Center for Disaster
Reduction Systems, Disaster
Prevention Research Institute,
Kyoto University + GK Kyoto.
    Design: GK Kyoto Inc
    Designer: Kenshin Urabe

©PICTO-KEN
1999, All right reserved.

03, 04
www.howies.com
designed by
Carter Wong Tomlin

'HOW MANY OF
YOUR DESIGN HEROES
HAVE CONTRIBUTED
ANYTHING
TO THE DEBATE?'

If you haven't had a look already, the website of the UK-based clothes retailer Howies is well worth a visit. Proudly based in Cardigan, in west Wales, Howies is one of those businesses that grew out of the passion of one or two people. In this case, it was mountain biking and skateboarding. For a few years it was an enjoyable sideline for the owners, but now Howies is starting to take off. It boasts a catalogue, a website and a full range of gear, from t-shirts and fleeces to jeans, jackets and hats, that has just been launched at Selfridges in London.

03

www.howies.co.uk, which was designed by London design group Carter Wong Tomlin, conveys perfectly the redoubtable, lust-for-life philosophy of the Howies team. Everything is presented in a fashionably utilitarian visual style, allowing the clothes, the philosophy and the correlations between them, to shine brightly.

The highlight for me (never having straddled a BMX) is the Truth Index, where the 'grow slow', live-for-today credo reflected in designs and slogans on Howies' clothes is given substance by animated information graphics. There's a Howies clock, which breaks the day into 86,400 seconds and counts them down, one by one, as you watch. There's a Journey To Work barchart that records the CO_2 generated during a typical trip to the office by different modes of transport (including kayak). And there's an eye-opening 'Fubar' graphic, which traces the tortuous paths taken by food transporters to bring the ingredients of a supermarket's chicken casserole by road from across Europe to the UK.

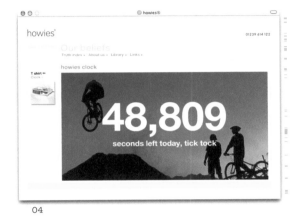

04

It all does the job of portraying Howies as a company that cares but knows how to have a blast. But it's more than mere infotainment. Visually engaging without ever indulging in what Edward Tufte would call 'chartjunk', the Truth Index infographics make their point with a minimum of fuss and a lot of style. In contrast to so many charts, graphs and diagrams seen in corporate annual reports, which are dressed up and pulled in all directions to compensate for their lack of engaging data, the Howies infographics deliver data in a plain, authoritative fashion, leaving the statistics to make their own compelling argument.

Browsing the Howies site, one suddenly becomes aware of how poorly information and data about environmental issues is communicated elsewhere, in print and online. Engagement between the environmental movement and top quality graphic design has been minimal. When was the last time anything with an environmental theme came close to winning a D&AD Silver or Gold? How many of your design heroes have contributed anything to the debate?

Memorable contributions are few and far between, and limited to the realm of self-expression and rhetoric. The mutation of the ESSO logo into E$$O by Greenpeace and others, in protest at the oil company's stand on global warming, was a rare flash of inspiration in a visually turgid field. The late Tibor Kalman's use in Colors 13 of stock aerial and landscape photography to encapsulate, without words, the beauty and vulnerability of the planet, was typically impassioned.

But in terms of design that packages environmental information in ways that ordinary, uncommitted consumers might want to explore, it's a pretty barren landscape.

Could it be that the environment is no longer seen as a cool topic for design? Perhaps some think it's not much of an issue anymore. How the ozone layer or the rain forests or the world's animal species could do with the cool value – and the publicity – generated by (former Kalman protegé) Stefan Sagmeister for the Move Our Money campaign. MOM started out (pre 9/11) with a specific intention: that of persuading the US Government to switch 15% of its defence budget of £310 billion to education and healthcare. MOM founder Ben Cohen (of Ben & Jerry fame) asked designer-of-the-moment Sagmeister to help raise support for the campaign. Instead of a logo, Sagmeister came up with a set of simple graphs and charts quantifying the ludicrous scale of military funding, which were then applied to t-shirts, mugs, pens and inflatable structures (http://www.sagmeister.com/work14.html).

Anyone who doubts the urgency for a similarly fresh, honest approach to the communication of eco-related imbalances should be reminded of the dizzying speed of recent environmental reverses in the US. Since the late 1980s, when widespread concern arose about ozone depletion, global warming and pollution, public knowledge of the environmental crisis has been subject to confusion and deception by corporations with their profits threatened by new regulations. Every available public relations technique and information technology has been deployed in the battle of ideas with environmental groups. In the US, this billion dollar investment has been rewarded with the installation of George W Bush in the White House – a true enemy of nature.

Bush makes Ronald Reagan seem like the environment's best buddy. Not content with conflict on crude-rich foreign territory, the former Texas oiler has also been waging war on home soil – on its soil, its air and its water, to be exact. In his three years in office, Bush has overseen a stream of measures that manifestly favour corporate interests over the public interest, and unravelled environmental protections that in the past 30 years have gone some way to improving the quality of life for Americans.

A key part of his programme has been the masterful miscommunication of initiatives and proposals, and the use of environmental spin, or 'greenwash'. The naming of proposals and initiatives with catchy two-word titles that apply a positive gloss and stick in the mind is a skill Bush advisors have honed to perfection. Hence, we have an initiative designed to weaken long-standing limits on pollution from coal-fired power stations given the name of 'Clear Skies', and a measure that allows logging companies to move into previously protected woodlands that's called 'Healthy Forests'. According to the US environmental magazine Mother Jones, 'Clear Skies' would lead to an extra 42 million tonnes of air pollutants being released over US towns and cities by 2020.

Hand in hand with greenwashing, the White House has suppressed reports from official sources about environmental crises. A document from the government's own Environmental Protection Agency warning of the health risks (including neurological damage) to children of mercury emissions from coal-fired power plants was sat on for nine months, according to the

Inside /
Ungraphic Environment

Inside /
page 163

Inside /
Essay

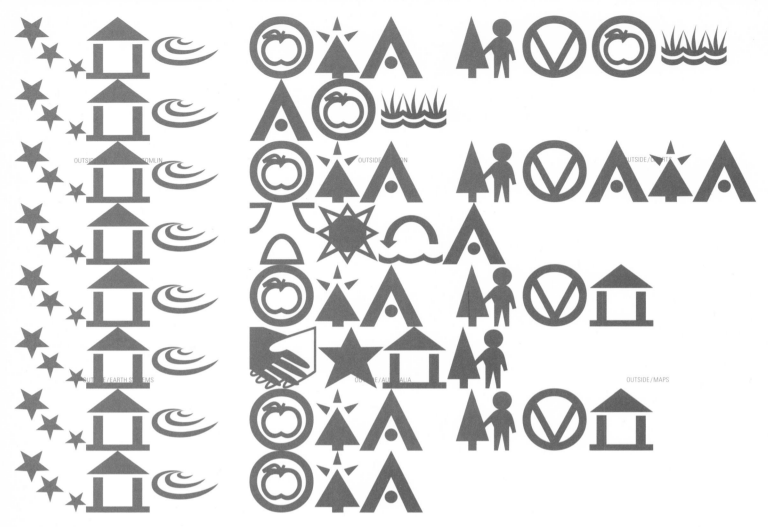

Wall Street Journal in 2003, while the 'Clear Skies' programme was honed and launched. Activists are appalled to find that the combination of 'greenwash' terminology and the suppression of inconvenient research is having an influence on public perceptions of environmental policies.

While public knowledge is being manipulated in this manner and while the natural world continues to suffer there remains an urgent need for facts about environmental threats to be communicated with more immediacy. The facts are there and they are terrifying (climate change to kill off one in ten animal and plant species by 2050, by the way, according to a recent comprehensive study on four continents). Relaying them in down-the-page newspaper reports may not be enough to sustain the average person's commitment to environmental causes. Relating the facts to their own experience in a visually accessible form might be.

The shortage of really well-designed environmental information may partly be explained by the newness of the challenges associated with phenomena like climate change. Humanity is still coming to terms with the destruction it has caused. How do you signpost knowledge when that knowledge is developing with each passing month? We are still in the early stages of learning what the implications are of each crisis, and what our response should be. In truth, though, in terms of influencing behaviour, we can't hang around. We do know a great deal more about what's happening to the planet now than we did 15, 10 or five years ago, and design can – must – help to communicate that knowledge.

There have been intriguing attempts to get to grips in print with this ballooning of information. Two of these are the World Environment Map, produced by Australian consultants Earth Systems, and the State of the World Atlas, designed by Myriad Editions of Brighton and published by Earthscan. The map is an attempt to provide an impartial 'snapshot of the world's environment'. It's an extraordinary assembly of data and information from numerous sources onto a single sheet of paper. Crowded onto the 1300mm by 900mm wall map are countless notes about environmental issues and concerns (oil spills, nuclear accidents, deforestation etc.) and information about green initiatives and achievements. Then, along the top and bottom of the map are arrays of charts and graphs revealing trends and geographical comparisons in areas such as water, biodiversity, waste and land use.

'There is definitely a lack of highly technical, factually accurate environmental information presented in a way which is accessible to more people without the need for the internet, or software knowledge,' says Earth Systems' Catherine Oke. 'By presenting information on a map, people can also get a spatial representation of a range of environmental information, and hopefully put into perspective what is happening around the world, how it affects them, and how they affect the environment.'

It won't win any design awards and its density is daunting, but the World Environment Map remains an amazing achievement whose spirit of objectivity and public education might inspire those with a more finely-tuned visual and editorial sense. The State of the World Atlas and its related titles (The Atlas of the Environment and The Atlas of Food among them) show, on the other hand, the benefit of strong, judicious editing and resourceful information design. Each spread presents a statistical map or 'cartogram' that tells a story about an issue in a way that's compelling and razor sharp. 'A single map here tells us more about the world today than a dozen abstracts or scholarly tomes,' said the Los Angeles Times about the Atlas.

Environmental change is generating new challenges for design, and there are instances emerging of these being met by the adaptation of familiar design applications. Take the efforts made by a multidisciplinary team in Japan (which included design group GK Kyoto) to develop a system of permanent street signs

Inside /
Ungraphic Environment

Inside /
page 164

Inside /
Essay

Tsunami

Tsunami Warning

Protect life from a Tsunami

If an earthquake came · · ·

In case of earthquake, go to high ground or over 3rd stiries building.

Tsunami refuge place、
Tsunami refuge building、 (A safe place)

Leave the sea and a river.

The high tournament please take refuge than the 3rd floor of a building

THIS PAGE:
Japan National Commitee for IDNDR Pictogram Project (PICTO-KEN). Pictogram system for Natural Disaster Reduction produced in collaboration with the Research Center for Disaster Reduction Systems, Disaster Prevention Research Institute, Kyoto University + GK Kyoto.
   Design: GK Kyoto Inc
   Designer: Kenshin Urabe

PREVIOUS PAGE:
Green Map System Icons
© 2004 Green Map™ System, Inc.

for certain Pacific-facing resorts, intended to offer evacuation directions in the event of a tsunami ('great wave') attack.

Devised with an actual town in mind on Shikoku Island where the beach attracts large crowds of tourists, the programme included signboards at the railway station and harbour alerting visitors to the threat, electronic roadsigns showing evacuation directions when tremors over a certain magnitude are registered, and street signs on poles recording how high previous waves had been (thereby indicating a safe height at which to shelter inside buildings). It may not do the local tourist industry a lot of good, but this system is the first of its kind and creates a template that other threatened areas might utilise, especially since our off-balance environment is throwing up natural catastrophes at an increasing rate (weather-related catastrophes cost the world $60 billion in 2003, according to the UN). In fact, the system was developed in response to the UN's designation of the 1990s as the 'International Decade for Natural Disaster Reduction'.

A different kind of information design response to the environmental crisis – or, rather, to the eco-cultural boom it has engendered – is the Green Map System (http://www.greenmap.org/). Taken up by designers in cities on every continent, the GMS comprises a set of icons denoting environmental resources and attractions, from farmers' markets and Fair Trade shops to conservation sites, information centres and bicycle routes. Pictograms for environmental blackspots are also included. With the consent of the GMS developers, designers are free to overlay the icons on a map of his or her own city or area, and thereby create their own local Green Map.

It's a wonderfully simple but powerful idea with positive spin-offs all round. Green enterprises are promoted and supported, and communities become aware of the facilities available in their midst. Green Maps have helped to sustain ecologically sound cafés and farmers, shops, services and construction projects. Notes-swapping between groups of mapmakers have led to innovative greening initiatives being replicated from city to city. At the last count there was well in excess of 220 Green Map projects – in print and online – active in 40 countries. It's a rare example of design democracy in action: every Map is different, each one has its own local flavour. The visual and cultural diversity across the collection is unique.

The GMS, by utilising a form of information design familiar and accessible to all, widens its audience enormously. 'Our network includes projects in rural areas and small villages as well as capital cities and urbanised towns,' says the GMS's originator, Wendy Brawer. 'Many of the two million copies of locally-created Green Maps are designed in a way to reach those who might not pick up and use any other kind of eco-information. Using maps as our

'HUMANITY IS STILL COMING TO TERMS WITH THE DESTRUCTION IT HAS CAUSED. HOW DO YOU SIGNPOST KNOWLEDGE WHEN THAT KNOWLEDGE IS DEVELOPING WITH EACH PASSING MONTH?'

Inside /
Ungraphic Environment

Inside /
page 165

Inside /
Essay

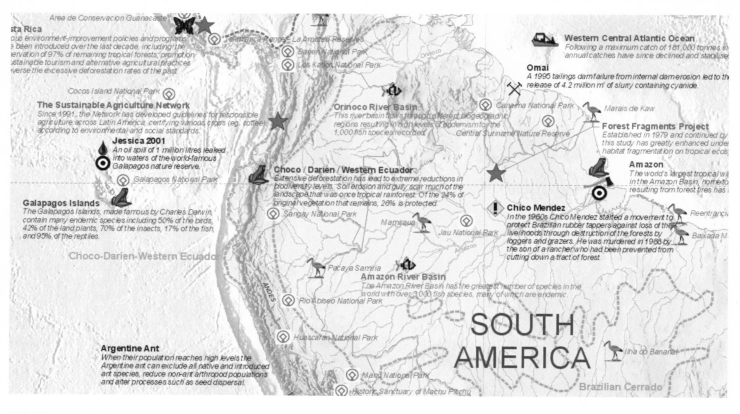

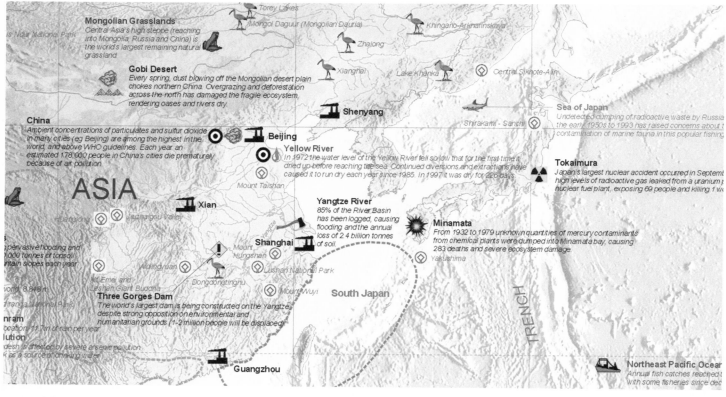

THIS PAGE:
World Environment Map (Details)
produced by
Earth Systems

Inside /
Ungraphic Environment

Inside /
page 166

Inside /
Essay

'...IT IS TO VISUAL COMMUNICATORS AND GRAPHIC DESIGNERS THAT WE MUST LOOK IF VITAL MESSAGES ABOUT THE DETERIORATING STATE OF OUR PLANET ARE NOT TO BE LOST COMPLETELY IN A SEA OF HYPERBOLE AND DOUBLETALK.'

'GRAPHIC DESIGN, AT ITS BEST, BRINGS TO THE SURFACE THE INFORMATION AND IDEAS THAT CAN CHANGE MINDS. IT MAKES VISIBLE WHAT WAS UNSEEN.'

medium gives us an advantage, because people really like to look at their home, and Green Maps can give them a new worldview that recovers long-lost connections to community and nature.'

Exactly the same premise underlies the success of Scorecard, the environmental organisation that provides the dark flipside to the Green Map and discloses to US citizens – in frighteningly accessible form – the eco-hazards on their doorstep. Scorecard integrates environmental data from 400 scientific and governmental sources. Go to http://www.scorecard.org/ and you'll find a home page that provides an instant snapshot of America's most polluted states. Roll your mouse over headings such as 'Lead Hazards' or 'Animal Waste From Factory Farms' and the rash on the credit card-sized US map changes colour and distribution to reflect the relevant data.

If what you see alarms you (say, if you live in Detroit, and are looking at the map of 'Toxic Releases From Industrial Facilities'), within a couple of clicks you can be at a bar chart that ranks Illinois nationally in terms of delights such as air releases of recognised reproductive toxicants (Illinois is in the nation's worst 10% of states) and air releases of recognised carcinogens (again, Illinois is among the dirtiest 10%). All kinds of state-specific data is there. Better still, you can enter your zip code and get a detailed breakdown of your own district's environmental performance. A million attempted hits on the website within 24 hours of its launch in 1998 tells its own story about the demand for dependable information about local environmental conditions.

Scorecard is an exception. As environmental groups go, it is unique in coupling data to design in such an engaging, easy-to-access form. As Brawer says of the Green Map System (although she might be speaking for the green movement as a whole): 'We need better designers to get involved to continually widen our sphere of influence.' Which returns us to the central point: the need for more designers and organisations to follow the examples of Scorecard and the GMS, and adapt established, familiar visual communication systems to widen access to environmental information.

If there are graphic designers out there looking for a new, meaningful purpose, they could hardly choose better. In graphic design's customary state, as a compliant, passive purveyor of corporate ideologies and images, opportunities for disclosing unattractive facts about environmental change are few and far between. Howies isn't your average client. Yet it is to visual communicators and graphic designers that we must look if vital messages about the deteriorating state of our planet are not to be lost completely in a sea of hyperbole and doubletalk. We need to rediscover the spirit and intentions of Otto Neurath, the Viennese philosopher and social scientist who in the 1930s developed the Isotype system of pictograms (now more familiar in public information signs) to act as symbols in revolutionary charts that educated the public about society, culture and economics.

Environmental groups in need of a stronger, more popular voice have to employ more visually inventive techniques to communicate the facts about environmental degradation. Mainstream organisations like Greenpeace may have sidelined themselves permanently by failing to match their corporate and industrial foes in packaging environmental information accessibly. At www.greenpeace.org, for example, you'll find acres of text about PVC products, PVC waste, PVC recycling, PVC landfills, PVC incineration and so on. It's all good, solid, informative stuff. In the midst of it we read this: 'There are currently over 150 million tonnes of long-life PVC materials in existence globally.' Sounds a lot doesn't it? But we can't picture it. This gem of information about consumer waste is itself wasted because our brains are too busy trying to compare 150 million tonnes to something whose weight we can appreciate.

We'd get a closer idea of what 150 million tonnes of non-biodegradable plastic looked like if Greenpeace had a policy of turning its awesome statistics into something more tangible and immediate. Howies' Truth Index includes a page where the weight of plastic bottles disposed of in the UK is measured in units of B-52 bombers. As a counter clocks up the number of bottles bought each day, in real time – at a speed faster than the eye can see – a set of fawn-coloured B-52 silhouettes slowly fill up dark brown.

It's inexorable; the true scale and relentlessness of waste in our culture begins to become apparent. At midnight, when the sixth plane has completely changed colour, the cycle starts again, and another six B-52s await their cargo of garbage. Howies is a small fashion retailer; it isn't Greenpeace, Friends of the Earth nor any kind of campaigning organisation, yet its (and Carter Wong Tomlin's) selection and visual presentation of environmental statistics provides a model that those bodies could do well to learn from. (If it helps, 150 million tonnes is roughly what 6000 Titanics would weigh).

Graphic design, at its best, brings to the surface the information and ideas that can change minds. It makes visible what was unseen. Graphic designers, working with other communicators and experts, can engineer and foster wider understanding of complex matters. And there is no matter more complex – nor one more in need of greater understanding – than the environment.

* * *

Michael Evamy is the author of World Without Words, a survey of the modern boom in wordless visual communication, published by Laurence King.

LINKS:
www.howies.com
www.sagmeister.com
www.greenmap.org
www.scorecard.org

Inside /
Ungraphic Environment

Inside /
page 167

Inside /
Essay

Been There Done That

writing by
Rosanna Vitiello

01

The cult object is becoming obsolete. It seems everyone wants a life full of designer goods, but as this becomes the norm, these products inevitably lose their sparkle. No, what's really de-rigeur nowadays is a collection of cult experiences; you're no one without a gap year, bungee jump or track-racing day under your belt.

As testament to this, luxury goods sales have dropped dramatically over the past year, in large part due to global recession. However, as we tighten our purse strings we have also become more selective, questioning the lasting value of what we're paying for. It's considered more fulfilling and less superficial to spend the money on, say, a trekking holiday rather than a designer bag of equal value. In buying an experience, we're rewarded with a beneficial, long-term effect in the form of an adrenalin rush, a sense of achievement or most importantly, a happy memory. The paradox is that these are relatively instantaneous events, the physical life of which is much shorter than a tangible good. After all, your handbag will be out of fashion next season, but you'll want to tell your grandchildren about your Himalayan trek.

It hasn't taken long for the commercial world to realise that the highest priority on our shopping list is now an experience. To make the most of this (and to counteract falling sales) businesses are attempting to work experiences into the packages they offer us. Termed the 'Experience Economy', this shows how economics has moved a step beyond the service industries, to the provision of experiences. So, for instance, McDonald's will not only serve you a burger, they'll put on a birthday party for your child, and give you a happy meal toy as a 'souvenir' to prolong the memory.

The retail sector, in particular, has gone to town on the experience economy. Selfridges' former CEO, Vittorio Radice, revived the dusty department store, creating one of the most desirable shopping destinations in the world that, critically,

01
Droog Design:
'Do Hit' chair (2000)
Designer: Marijn van der Poll,
1.25mm steel, hammer
100x70x75cm
Photography: Bianca Pilet

02
Blur Building
Pavilion at the 2002 Swiss
Expo, Neuchatel.
Architects: Diller & Scofidio

'IT'S ONLY A SHORT STEP TOWARDS DESIGNERS BUILDING EXPERIENCES INTO THEIR CREATIONS, OR INDEED, CREATING EXPERIENCES THEMSELVES'

is equally open to all. His aim was to transform the whole process of visiting Selfridges into an all-consuming experience, not just a shopping trip. Hence a series of highly successful mini-festivals such as Tokyo Life and Body Craze, in which, amongst other events, 600 naked people rode up and down the escalators. This is proving a successful strategy. Sales increased by 10.6% over the past year.

Radice has recently moved to high-street retailer Marks & Spencer, developing the concept of the 'Lifestore'. Here, products are grouped together under lifestyle headings such as Cook, Renew, Relax, Escape, Play and Celebration, a direct indication of the shift towards the experience and away from the product.

Design has a tendency to draw from the culture that surrounds it, so it's only a short step towards designers building experiences into their creations, or indeed, creating experiences themselves. The Design Academy Eindhoven has run Funlab, an MA in Experience and Entertainment design, since 2000. Through 'dismantling the seniority of the object',

Inside /
Been There, Done That

Inside /
page 168

Inside /
Writing

Funlab's ultimate aim is to 'activate the audience to join in, participate and then leave transformed by a meaningful experience'. The fact that there is even demand for this course is indicative of a shift in design over the past five years. Products are increasingly imbued with a human quality that in some way engages and interacts with us, providing an experience. Such designs give a sense that what we create doesn't have to be tangible; most importantly it should somehow clutch onto our emotions. The beauty is that in doing so, designers are turning the rejection of cult products directly on its head, embracing the sought-after experience. So now you can have your cake (the product) and eat it (the experience).

Product design has been a natural opening for this, since it heavily involves human interaction. Going way beyond any self-assembly furniture we've seen before, Dutch Droog Design and ad agency Kessels Kramers collaborated on 'do create', a series of products that require you to do something to them to complete the design. As Renny Ramakers of Droog puts it: 'Rather than being tacked on, an experience lies in the product's intrinsic quality as brought to bear by the product itself'. Take 'Do Hit', a chair supplied as a metal cube accompanied by a sledgehammer. The buyer has to bash the hell out of the metal until they've created just the right shape to recline in. There's an element of instant attachment that goes beyond an IKEA flat pack, because each piece is unique, being customised by the buyer. And because there is a sense of 'I made this' satisfaction involved in the product's creation, each piece becomes highly memorable.

In some instances the product reacts to the user, rather than the user having to react to the product. Designers Will Cary, Natasha Chetiyawardana and Stijjn Ossevort recently collaborated on 'Seen the light,' a range of interactive lighting products which gain meaning from participation. Amongst the products is 'memo', a light which remembers energy as it flows though it. When switched off, the light cable and inside of the shade glow, showing the energy expended when the light was on. Another, 'Still life,' starts off as an apparently blank wall canvas, but reacts to movement as people walk past, activating lights or pulsating if a mobile phone is in the vicinity. Although seemingly inanimate, these products begin to develop a relationship with the user, and we start to recognise the qualities we enjoy in them. They experience us as much as we experience them.

Architecture plays with experience on a much larger scale, with the advantage of creating all-encompassing environments. In designing the Jewish Museum in Berlin, Daniel Libeskind intended to evoke the pain of the Holocaust era, creating a sombre building of dark corners and staircases leading to nowhere. He toys with our emotional sensibilities, allowing us to experience the confusion and bleakness directly in an attempt to better understand the subject. According to Liebeskind's philosophy, 'a building can be experienced as an unfinished journey. It can awaken our desires, propose imaginary conclusions. It is not about form, image or text, but about the experience, which is not to be simulated.'

But an experience doesn't have to be delivered in the form of a concrete object. New York based practice, Diller and Scofidio, created what they describe as the 'formless, featureless…massless' Blur pavilion for the sixth Swiss Expo in 2002. It was, in effect, a man-made cloud, hovering over Lake Neuchatel. Over 30,000 jets on a suspended platform sprayed droplets of lake water to create the shroud of mist. Visitors were provided with 'brain coats', technologically enhanced raincoats that reacted to each other through colour changes and sound. The unique experience of walking through a cloud takes centre stage here, the intangible nature of the 'building' itself acting almost as a backdrop.

The blur building is a step towards the pinnacle of designing experiences: to almost disregard the product in

02

favour of the experience itself. Marieje Van Buuren and Eva Helberger's 'Shadows of Desire' project completely does away with the product, focussing instead on the experience of ownership. A series of thick felt 'shadows' of cult products, such as a Vernor Panton chair or a Patek Phillipe watch, can be selected from the catalogue, and laid on the floor or hung on the wall. Categorised as 'shadows of taste,' 'shadows of success' or 'shadows of love', they provide the caché and sensation of living with such desirable products at a fraction of the price of the real thing. Of course they're a visual joke; an ironic take on the inevitable trap of the fake (literally a shadow of the real thing). The commoditisation of designer products has led to a surge in fake or diluted versions of designer goods. Now that we're obsessed with experiences, does it follow that we'll make compromises in quality, in an attempt to cross another one off our 'to do' lists?

The tourism and entertainment industries have long offered an array of diluted versions of reality. Las Vegas has become the epicentre of what's described as 'Entertainment Architecture'; at various themed hotels along the strip, you can get a taste of a plastic New York, Paris, Cairo and Venice all within walking distance. Glenn Schaeffer, CEO of Circus Circus (the world's biggest gaming corporation), commented on how he'd once heard a tourist standing in front of the medieval Excalibur resort who said: 'Well, I don't have to go to England. No – I've seen it all right here in Las Vegas.' Complete with an animatronic dragon that roars every hour, of course. But the tourist was right; there really is no need to go so far nowadays. We can pop to our local WH Smith to pick up a packaged experience off the shelf, anything from sushi schools to shark dives. Such packages allow us to be someone else and somewhere else for a day. But they are life's version of a ready meal; accessible, quick and easy, but essentially not as satisfying as the real thing. Herein lies the problem; it all becomes too easy. The second time you experience something, it will become marginally less enjoyable than the first, the third time even more so. Experiences are being thrown at us in every sphere of life; shopping, holidays, products, TV. These sensations are becoming increasingly everyday.

Yet what we really want out of an experience is a change from the daily grind. After all, who would buy into 'a day at the office' or 'a day of housework'? This would suggest another shift is about to take place in the experience industry. The paradigm experience would give us more than just change, but total transformation; not just changing our mood, but altering our very being as the buyer. Such life changing experiences might include a visit to a life coach, a makeover, or a religious retreat. However, this switches our relationship with the experience itself. In offering us a transformation there is no tangible product to sell; nothing new. The difference lies in that when we buy into the transformation, ripe and ready for a life changing experience, the product on offer is actually ourselves.

* * *

Inside /
Been There, Done That

Inside /
page 169

Inside /
Writing

Passed Places

writing by
James Davis

01

Innocent but unloved stairwells, undulating plains of paving stone. Brittle ledges draw the eye to long demolished carbuncles; accidental vertices protrude from concrete glaciers, optimistic squares cling to long-disproved commercial promises; sealed courtyards glimpsed only through the dirty rear windows of a post room; car-park stalactites drip methodically onto SLOW signs painted on a carpet of ribbed, beige concrete. Aggressive moss suffocates a once proud fleet of red bricks arranged with amateur artistry into a hull-shape at the base of a tax office. A mellow wooden wheelchair ramp tramples its cement predecessor, demoted for inclining too steeply. The endless metal of a low railing serves only to lengthen the route of those unable to hop the shortcut; earth spills from a cracked flowerbed speckled by plants struggling with the dark grey dust; a stubby metal pole heralds the centre of the entrance to an entirely-vacated office complex; urine gathers into dark, slimy mounds at the periphery of peripheries.

These spaces, jettisoned by our need for 'better' locations, often stand as ugly obstacles to our destination.

Environmental oddities are often designed badly enough, or weathered extremely enough, or forced out of context so far as to exist better in roles for which the architect did not intend; at least for city-dwellers whose navigation of the city is not based on location but interpretation. They are burglars, wheelchair users, tramps, skateboarders, prostitutes, taxi-drivers, children, wild animals, fly-tippers, illegal traders and graffiti artists who find tempting aspects of this poisoned palate.

This experience begins with the city, at the outskirts. Here we find transport limbs corrupting the verge of the greenbelt, the abrasion between demeaned farmland and debased urban work zones. The eye – startled out of its involuntary and commercial oscillations – begins to focus on a certain physical ether, as if redirecting peripheral vision to the fore. Only then do we notice the corners. The dark corners. The bits in the way. The ugly stuff. The spaces that exist neither by accident nor design, but by fresh contexts demanding recognition in this self-conscious reality. Lines of perspective meet in the finest of wrong places. Incompatible textures suffer hideous arranged marriages, yet beauty somehow emerges. The shades of grey blend and reverberate, echo and reflect; this complexity passed on to the viewer, now able to determine nuances of tone in the two thousand slabs they pass on the way to the bus stop.

Inside /
Passed Places

Inside /
page 170

Inside /
Writing

01, 02
Passed Places
Spaces in London.
Photographs by James Davis

02

'LINES OF PERSPECTIVE
MEET IN THE FINEST
OF WRONG PLACES.
INCOMPATIBLE TEXTURES
SUFFER HIDEOUS
ARRANGED MARRIAGES,
YET BEAUTY SOMEHOW
EMERGES'

What's good about the city is what's bad about the city.
There is inspiration to be found in the disasters of visionary
incompetence. Road signs in groups of a dozen become a comical
brigade: useless to the motorist, offensive to the aesthete, but
strangely and appropriately redolent of our stupid culture. A
touching quiff of primary-coloured earnestness; naive as a
kindergarten landscape. When we begin to look at the lines
created by this erroneous distribution, we glimpse a new type
of perspective. Unconcerned with physical reality, dimensions
are formed by, say, the eroded texture of a propped plywood
sheet in the afternoon sunshine. An oily puddle reflects the
image of the eye of a four metre tall underwear model glued to
the side of a double-decker. Beneath her elbow a lady, dressed
as a woman in a knitted hat, leans her head against a window
scratched with the word FOXY. As the bus passes by, the filthy
but still fluorescent bolt-positioners spin round on the wheels,
gesturing towards a red line painted atop a yellow line painted
atop a Victorian drain embedded in a resurfaced street. The
image is impossibly complex and natural, yet totally false,

ugly and understandably ignored by most. They've got buses to
catch, after all. You couldn't design it if you tried. We can only
hope to recognise the symptoms of this visual back-end through
our perceptual acuity. And perhaps emulate some of its more
successful iterations in the way we reintroduce this world into
our design.

The glib painting of shadows on the street or the middle-
class anarchy of cleaning dirty buildings without permission
represents the first thimble of this idea. But can we hope for
less-sincere development? Dare we imagine a sealed world of
thoughtful but non-ironic abstractions emerging from such
playful behaviour?

If much of visual design is about plagiarism of our
surroundings, then perhaps we can return the favour towards
our environment. Distribute conceptual aids to this end
throughout the city – a warm mocking through contextual
design – effecting a silvery moiré blanket to project influence
onto those non-spaces. The viscera – previously emitted by
these locations but translated into little more than stress
– is now free for more productive engagement, like a 1983
videogame arcade experience. Abstract valleys emerge between
the city's high-points of cultural importance; perhaps we can
live in-between, without a need for our supposed destinations.
It's an attractive route really, and someone's already begun to
paint it pink.

* * *

Cover printed on
250 g/m² Luxocard I

SCHNEIDER
PAPIER

PEOPLE AND PAPER

B. Bird

www.zefa.co.uk 020.7079 0540
rights managed and royalty free imagery

z|e|f|a

GRAPHIC is distributed by:

Australia
Tower Books
Unit 2, 17 Rodborough Road
Frenchs Forest, NSW 2086
T +62 2 9975 5566
F +62 2 9975 5599
E towerbks@zipworld.com.au
www.foliograph.com.au

Belgium
Bookstores
Exhibitions International
Kol. Begaultlaan 17
B-3012 Leuven
T +32 16 296 900
F +32 16 284 540
E orders@exhibitionsinternational.be
www.exhibitionsinternational.be

Other
Imapress
Brugstraat 51
B-2300 Turnhout

China
Beijing Zhong Ke I/E Company of China Science
Publishing Group
16 Dong Huangchenggen North Street
Beijing 100717
T 010-6406 7653
F 010-6406-0931
E citbooks@x263.net

France
Critique Livres Distribution SAS
BP 93-24 rue Malmaison
93172 Bagnolet Cedex
T +33 1 4360 3910
F +33 1 4897 3706
E critiques.livres@wanadoo.fr

Germany
Bookstores
Sales representative South Germany:
Stefan Schempp
Augsburger Strasse 12
D-80337 München
T +49 89-230 77 737
F +49 89-230 77 738
E verlagsvertretung.schempp@t-online.de

North Germany
Sales Representative
Kurt Salchli
Marienburger Strasse 10
D-10405 Berlin
T +49 30 4171 7530
F +49 30 4171 7531
E salchli@t-online.de

Germany, Austria & Switzerland
Distribution /Auslieferung
GVA Gemeinsame Verlagsauslieferung Göttingen
Anna-Vandenhoeck-Ring 36
37081 Göttingen
Germany
T +49 551 487 177
F +49 051 413 92
E krause@gva-verlage.de

Other
IPS Pressevertrieb GmbH
Carl-Zeiss-Strasse 5
D-53340 Meckenheim
T +49 22 258801 122
F +49 22 258801 199
E publishing@ips-pressevertrieb.de
www.ips-pressevertrieb.de

Indonesia
Aksara
Jalan Kemang Raya 8b
Jakarta 12730
T +62 21 7199 288
F +62 21 7199 282
E info@aksara.com
www.aksara.com

Italy
Idea srl
Via Lago Transimeno, 23/2 (ZI)
36015 Schio (VI)
T +39 455 576 574
F +39 445 577 764
E info@ideabooks.it
www.ideabooks.it

Red Edizioni Sas
Viale Prampolini 110
41100 Modena
T +39 59 212 792
F +39 59 4392 133
E info@redonline.it

Japan
Shimada Yosho
T.Place, 5-5-25, Minami-Aoyama, Minato-Ku
Tokyo, 107-0062
T +81 3 3407 3937
F +81 3 3407 0989
E sales@shimada.attnet.ne.jp

Korea
Beatboy Inc.
Kangnam-Ku Shinsa-Dong 666-11
Baegang Building 135-897
Seoul
T +82 3 3444 8367
F +82 2 541 8358
E yourbeatboy@hanmail.net

Malaysia
How & Why Sdn Bhd
101A, Jalan SS2/24
47300 Petaling Jaya
Selangor
T +60 3 7877 4800
F +60 3 7877 4600
E info@howwwhy.com
www.howwwhy.com

Mexico
LHR Distribuidor de Libros
Calle 11 No. 69-1
Col.V. Gomez Farias Mexico
D.F. 15010 Mexico
T +52 55 5785 8996
F +52 55 5785 7816
E lhrlibro@prodigy.net.mx
www.lhrlibros.com

The Netherlands
Bookstores
Betapress BV
Burg. Krollaan 14
5126 PT Gilze
T +31 161 457 800
F +31 161 457 224

Other
BIS Publishers
Herengracht 370-372
1016 CH Amsterdam
T +31 20 524 7560
F +31 20 524 7557
E bis@bispublishers.nl
www.bispublishers.nl

Russia
Design Books
3 Maly Kislovsky Lane office 315
Moscow 103009
T +7 095 203 65 94
F +7 095 203 65 94

Scandinavia
(Denmark, Finland, Norway, Sweden)
Sales Representative
Bo Rudin
Box 5058
SE-165 11 Hasselby
Sweden
T +46 8 894 080
F +46 8 388 320
E rudins@swipnet.se

Singapore
Basheer Graphic Books
Block 231, Bain Street
#04-19 Bras Basah Complex
180231 Singapore
T +65 336 0810
F +65 334 1950

Page One Pte Ltd
20 Kaki Bukit View
Kaki Bukit Techpark II
415956 Singapore
T +65 744 2088
F +65 744 2088
E pageone@singnet.com.sg

Spain
ACTAR
Roca i Batlle 2 i 4
08023 Barcelona
T +34 93 418 77 59
F +34 93 418 67 07
E info@actar-mail.com
www.actar.es

Taiwan
Long Sea International Book Co.,Ltd.
1/F No. 204 Si Wei Rd
Taipei 106 Taiwan ROC
T +886 2 2706 6838
F +886 2 ,2706 6109
E thfang@ms16.hinet.net
www.longsea.co.tw

Hong Kong
The Grand Commercial Co
Flat B, 4/F Kam Mow Ind Bldg
44 Belcher's Street, Kennedy Town
T +852 2570 9639
F +852 2570 4665
E thegrand@icare.com.hk

Turkey
Evrensel Grafikir Yayincilik
Gulbahar Mahl
Gayret SK No:11
80300-01 Mecidiyekoy/Istanbul
T +90 212 356 7276
F +90 212 356 7278
E evrensely@superonline.com

United Kingdom
Bookstores
Airlift Book Company
8 The Arena
Mollison Avenue
Enfield, Middlesex EN3 7NL
T +44 20 8804 0400
F +44 20 8804 0044
E info@airlift.co.uk
www.airlift.co.uk

Other
Comag Specialist
Tavistock Works
Tavistock Road
West Drayton
Middlesex UB7 7QX
T +44 1895 433 800
F +44 1895 433 801
E andy.hounslow@comag.co.uk

USA/Canada
Lords USA Enterprises Inc
99-27 66th Avenue, Rego Park
New York, NY 11374
T +1 718 275 1919
F +1 718 275 2332
lordsusainc@aol.com www.lordsusa.com

USA/West Coast
Trucatriche
3800 Main Street Suite 8
Chula Vista, CA 91911
California
T +1 619 426 2690
F +1 619 426 2695
E info@trucatriche.com

Subscriptions to graphic
(all prices include airmail)

1 year (4 issues)
○ Europe EUR80/GBP55
○ USA/Canada USD105
○ Other countries USD125

2 years (8 issues)
○ Europe EUR149/GBP103
○ USA/Canada USD195
○ Other countries USD225

Students
(valid only with a copy of your
student registration form)

1 year (4 issues)
○ Europe EUR63/GBP43.50
○ USA/Canada USD90
○ Other countries USD100

Fax this form to:
+31 20 524 75 57

or send to:
graphic
Herengracht 370-372
1016 CH Amsterdam
The Netherlands

Payment (for prompt delivery please pay by credit card)
○ Please charge my: ○ Visa ○ AmEx ○ Euro/Master
○ Please invoice me/my company
(first issue will be sent on receipt of payment)

Mr/Ms	Name		Surname	
Card number			CVC-2 Code *	
Expiry date		Signature		
Company				
Address **				
City			Postcode/Zip	
Country			Telephone	
Email			Fax	

*: Please add your CVC-2 code (the last 3 digits of the number
printed on the signature strip on the back of your card) if paying by Mastercard.

**: Please also attach details of card billing address if different from delivery address.

code GR/BZ/04

A Revolution A Day Keeps The Therapist Away

A young man gets out of bed and, naked, reaches into a large drawer filled with clothes. He digs out a crumpled t-shirt. 'THE SUN DOES NOT KNOW IT IS A STAR' the t-shirt proclaims in red letters (available in white and pink, sizes XS, S, M, L and XL). He reaches in again. 'SHOP LOCAL' this one says, blue letters on a beige t-shirt (also available in red, sizes XS, S, M, L and XL). He tries again. 'Hold on to young ideas', the t-shirt tells him. He cannot locate Jonathan Barnbrook's 'ONLY JERKS WEAR LOGOS' in the drawer but he finds TDR's 'BUY ME!' and the Jetset's 'Keith, Mick, Bill, Charlie & Brian.' which he is happy to find as he thought he had lost it. The clothes drawer continues to deliver messages: 'I GO ALL THE WAY', 'AMERICA IS NOT COOL', 'I AM A VIRUS', 'ARMED ARTIST', 'BREAD NOT BOMBS' (appropriate over breakfast). A bear smiles at him, letting him know that, 'I'M ROCKING ON YOUR DIME'. Icons (Che Guevara, Bob Marley, Jesus Christ, Steve McQueen in The Getaway, Beatrice Dalle in Betty Blue…), song lyrics and all kinds of symbols (birds, trees, flowers, hands, doves…) pop in and out of that crowded drawer. The last one to come out says 'ANTI.' in white letters on a black t-shirt (also available in red and green, sizes XS, M, L, XL). He holds it up, still hesitating.

*   *   *

Every t-shirt is a small act of rebellion. A rebellion against stiff collars, against ironing-boards, against the constricting effect of clothes and fashions on our bodies, against the weather (on this rainy London morning), against seriousness, against class, against gender, against age. T-shirts have little in common with the fickle revolutions of fashion. They're not pompous, they're not outrageous, they're not chic. The t-shirt is the uniform of the dreamer, of the optimist, of the idealist. There's always something nostalgic and vaguely comical about wearing a t-shirt. Let's pretend it's still Summer outside, let's pretend we're still young and that our lives are still simple and free and that our arms are tanned and hairless. T-shirts flap in the wind like youthful dreams.

*   *   *

Our generation has lived through a new kind of liberation. We have been liberated from politics, from the boring, old right-wing, left-wing dialectics. Terms such as 'bourgeois', 'proletarian', 'Marxist', 'Maoism', etc. shall soon be dropped from our dictionaries. And it's just as well. The answers are not in the lingo.

Now liberated from politics we can again become activists. We can forget that old profession and engage in discussions on moral and ethical grounds. The environment, globalisation, corporate power and accountability, the private sector vs the state, the religious vs the secular, monarchy vs republic, genetics, etc. The debate is no longer about left or right, but about right or wrong.

*   *   *

Imagine a man coming close to a window on the 38th floor of a high-security skyscraper. He does not open the window in order not to interfere with the air-conditioning of the flat, but takes up a pair of binoculars and directs them at the neighbouring shanty town, the favela, some 38 floors bellow. What you see looks at first like an immense junkyard. Then as he focuses his binoculars he starts noticing shapes, patterns – muddy dirt paths, a patchwork of corrugated iron sheets and boards and plastic and tarpaulin, fields of TV aerials, a door, a terrace, a vehicle – and only then he becomes aware of those dots moving between the other elements. These are the people, thousands of moving dots. What are they doing? What are their lives like? What do they feed on? What do they dream of? The man with the binoculars is like a scientist discovering a new form of life through a microscope. The man with the binoculars is aware of the fact that if he walks down to the shanty town nothing could prevent one of the ants from biting him. But he cannot help wondering what prevents the ants (there are millions of them, literally) from climbing up the skyscrapers waving axes?

*   *   *

Revolutions can have a lot to do with socio-economic backgrounds, but I believe that the driving force behind them is always cultural. There are only cultural revolutions. A revolution is inconceivable without a radical shift in perspective.

You can't launch a revolution with an advertising campaign. What matters is not what a slogan says or where the slogan is printed or pasted on, but how it resonates, how it echoes. Revolutions cannot be endorsed by personalities. Just think of Che Guevara's repeated failures (despite his already iconic status) in Africa and South America.

Revolutions come to the world like works of art. They grow in the dark, in the unconscious, first revealing themselves in sporadic sketches, which then suddenly, unexpectedly, assume their true (and often ghastly) shape and dimension.

The t-shirts in the drawer and the pages in the magazine are small pencil marks on a much greater canvas.

*   *   *

The t-shirt drawer stares at the naked young man like a crumpled demonstration. He makes up his mind and, wearing nothing but a slogan, stumbles towards the kitchen. 'You. Me. Us. Them. Now.' is available in S, M, L, XL. It glows in the dark.

*   *   *

Marc-A Valli

Inside /
Marc-A Valli

Inside /
page 176

Inside /
Afterword